Small Business Made Simple

Landlord Legal
Forms
Simplified

D1572772

Landlord Legal Forms Simplified

by Daniel Sitarz
Attorney-at-Law

Nova Publishing Company
Small Business and Consumer Legal Books and Software
Carbondale, Illinois

OCT   2007

ISBN 978-1-892949-24-0   Book w/CD   ($24.95)

Cataloging-in-Publication Data
Sitarz, Dan, 1948-
      Landlord legal forms simplified / by Daniel Sitarz. -- 1st ed. --
      Carbondale, Ill. : Nova Publishing, 2007.
      p. ; cm. + 1 CD-ROM.
      (Small business made simple)
      ISBN-13: 978-1-892949-24-0
      ISBN-10: 1-892949-24-5
      Includes index.
      1. Landlord and tenant--United States--Forms. 2. Real property--
      -United States--Forms. I. Title.
      KF588.1 .S58 2007
      346.7304/34--dc22 0708

b15174074

Nova Publishing Company is dedicated to providing up-to-date and accurate legal information to the public. All Nova publications are periodically revised to contain the latest available legal information.

1st Edition; 1st Printing: August, 2007

This publication is designed to provide accurate and authoritative information in regard to the subject matter covered. It is sold with the understanding that the publisher and author are not engaged in rendering legal, accounting, or other professional services. If legal advice or other expert assistance is required, the services of a competent professional person should be sought.

—From a Declaration of Principles jointly adopted by a Committee of the American Bar Association and a Committee of Publishers

DISCLAIMER

Nova Publishing Company
Small Business and Consumer Legal Books and Software
1103 West College St.
Carbondale, IL 62901
Editorial: (800) 748-1175
www.novapublishing.com

Distributed by:
National Book Network
4501 Forbes Blvd., Suite 200
Lanham, MD 20706
Orders: (800) 462-6420
www.nbnbooks.com

Nova Publishing Company Green Business Policies

Nova Publishing Company is committed to preserving ancient forests and natural resources. Our company's policy is to print all of our books on recycled paper, with no less than 30% post-consumer waste de-inked in a chlorine-free process. In addition, all Nova books are printed using soy-based inks. As a result, for the printing of this book, we have saved:

10.9 trees • 3,150 gallons of water • 1,845 kilowatt hours of electricity • 27 pounds of pollution

Nova Publishing Company is a member of Green Press Initiative, a nonprofit program dedicated to supporting publishers in their efforts to reduce their use of fiber obtained from endangered forests. For more information, go to www.greenpressinitiative.org. In addition, Nova uses all compact fluorescent lighting; recycles all office paper products, aluminum and plastic beverage containers, and printer cartridges; uses 100% post-consumer fiber, process-chlorine-free, acid-free paper for 95% of in-house paper use; and, when possible, uses electronic equipment that is EPA Energy Star-certified. Finally, all carbon emissions from office energy use are offset by the purchase of wind-energy credits that are used to subsidize the building of wind turbines on the Rosebud Sioux Reservation in South Dakota (see www.nativeenergy.com/coop).

Table of Contents

List of Forms-on-CD

All forms are provided in both PDF and text formats unless otherwise noted. PDF forms are fillable on a computer unless noted.

Residential Lease
Commercial Gross Lease
Commercial Net Lease
Lease with Purchase Option
Month to Month Rental Agreement
Amendment of Lease
Extension of Lease
Mutual Termination of Lease
Assignment of Lease
Consent to Assignment of Lease
Sublease
Consent to Sublease of Lease
Notice of Rent Default
Notice of Breach of Lease
Notice of Intent to Enter
Notice to Pay Rent or Vacate Property
Notice of Service Performed
Notice to Terminate Lease
Final Notice Before Legal Action
Notice of Approval of Tenant Alterations to Property
Notice of Lease
Rental Application (PDF version is not fillable on a computer)
Receipt for Lease Security Deposit
Notice of Denial of Rental Application
Lease Security Deposit Return Letter
Rent Receipt
Move-in/Move-out Checklist and Acknowledgment (PDF is not fillable on a computer)
Federal Lead Warning Brochure (PDF Only)

The following additional forms are provided:
California Addendum to Lease
Chicago Addendum to Lease
Chicago Heating Disclosure Form (PDF form only, not fillable on a computer)
Chicago Residential Landlord and Tenant Ordinance Summary (PDF form not fillable)
Florida Attachment to Lease Regarding Security Deposits

Preface

This book is part of Nova Publishing Company's continuing series on *Small Business Made Simple*. The various self-help legal guides in this series are prepared by licensed attorneys who feel that public access to the American legal system is long overdue.

Law in American society is far more pervasive than ever before. There are legal consequences to virtually every public and most private actions in today's world. Leaving knowledge of the law within the hands of only the lawyers in such a society is not only foolish, but dangerous as well. A free society depends, in large part, on an informed citizenry. This book and others in Nova's *Small Business Made Simple* series are intended to provide the necessary information to those members of the public who wish to use and understand the law for themselves.

However, in an area as complex as real estate rentals, encompassing topics as diverse as property law, landlord-tenant law, and legal contracts, it is not always prudent to attempt to handle every legal situation which arises without the aid of a competent attorney. Although the information presented in this book will give its readers a basic understanding of the areas of law covered, it is not intended that this text entirely substitute for experienced legal assistance in all situations. Throughout this book there are references to those particular situations in which the aid of a lawyer is strongly recommended.

Regardless of whether or not a lawyer is ultimately retained in certain situations, the legal information in this handbook will enable the reader to understand the framework of landlord-tenant law in this country and how to effectively use real estate forms in a wide variety of real estate rental transactions.

To try and make that task as easy as possible, technical legal jargon has been eliminated whenever possible and plain English used instead. Naturally, plain and easily understood English is not only perfectly proper for use in all legal documents but, in most cases, leads to far less confusion on the part of later readers. When it is necessary in this book to use a legal term which may be unfamiliar to most people, the word will be shown in *italics* and defined when first used.

CHAPTER 1
Using Landlord Legal Forms

The business arena in America operates on a daily assortment of legal forms. There are more legal forms in use in American business than are used in the operations and government of many foreign countries. Landlord/tenant transactions are not immune to this flood of legal forms. Unfortunately, many people who are confronted with such forms do not understand the legal ramifications of the use of these forms. They simply sign the lease, contract, or bill of sale with the expectation that it is a fairly standard document without any unusual legal provisions. They trust that the details of the particular document will fall within what is generally accepted within the industry or trade. In most cases, this may be true. In many situations, however, it is not. Our court system is clogged with cases in which two people are battling over what was really intended by the incomprehensible legal language in a certain contract.

Much of the confusion over business legal contracts comes from two areas. First, there is a general lack of understanding among many regarding the framework of contract law. Leases are simply a form of contract between a landlord and a tenant. Second, many leases are written in antiquated legal jargon that is difficult for most lawyers to understand and nearly impossible for a layperson to comprehend.

The leases and various legal documents that are used in this book are, however, written in plain English. Standard legal jargon, as used in most lawyer-prepared documents, is, for most people, totally incomprehensible. Despite the lofty arguments by attorneys regarding the need for such strained and difficult language, the vast majority of legalese is absolutely unnecessary. Clarity, simplicity, and readability should be the goal in legal documents.

Unfortunately, certain obscure legal terms are the only words that accurately and precisely describe some things in certain legal contexts. In those few cases, the unfamiliar legal term will be defined when first used. Generally, however, simple terms are used.

All of the legal documents contained in this book have been prepared in essentially the same manner that attorneys create legal forms. Many people believe that lawyers prepare each legal document that they compose entirely from scratch. Nothing could be further from the truth. Invariably, lawyers begin their preparation of a legal document with a standardized legal form book. Every law library has multi-volume sets of these encyclopedic texts that contain blank forms for virtually every conceivable legal situation. Armed with these pre-prepared legal forms, lawyers, in many cases, simply fill in the blanks and have their secretaries retype the form for the client. Of course, the client is generally unaware of this process.

This book provides the reader with a set of legal forms that has been prepared with the problems and issues of normal landlord/tenant transactions in mind. These forms are intended to be used in those situations that are clearly described by their terms. Of course, while most landlord/tenant transactions will fall within the bounds of standard business practices, some legal circumstances will present non-standard situations. The forms in this book are designed to be readily adaptable to most usual landlord/tenant situations. They may be carefully altered to conform to the particular transaction that confronts you. However, if you are faced with a complex or tangled landlord/tenant situation, the advice of a competent lawyer is recommended. If you wish, you may also create forms for certain standard landlord/tenant transactions and have your lawyer check them for any local legal circumstances.

The proper and cautious use of the forms provided in this book will allow the typical landlord to save considerable money on legal costs, while complying with legal and governmental regulations. Perhaps more important, these forms will provide a method by which the person can avoid costly misunderstandings about what exactly was intended in a particular situation or transaction. By using the forms provided to clearly set out the terms and conditions of everyday landlord/tenant dealings, disputes over what was really meant can be avoided. This protection will allow the reader to avoid many potential lawsuits and operate more efficiently in compliance with the law.

How to Use This Book

In each chapter of this book you will find an introductory section that will give you an overview of the types of situations in which the forms in that chapter will generally be used. Following that overview, there will be a brief explanation of the specific uses for each form. Included in the information provided for each form will be a discussion of the legal terms and conditions provided in the form. Finally, for each form, there is a listing of the information that must be compiled to complete the form.

The preferable manner for using these forms is to use the enclosed Forms-on-CD. Instructions for using the Forms-on-CD are included later in this chapter. However, it is perfectly acceptable to prepare these forms directly from the book by making a copy of the form, filling in the information that is necessary, and then retyping the form in its entirety on clean white letter-sized paper.

For purposes of simplification, most of the forms in this book are set out in a form as would be used by two individuals. However, any of the various forms can be adapted for use between two business entities or an individual and a business entity. If businesses are parties to the lease please identify the name and type of business entity (for example: Jackson Car Stereo, a New York sole proprietorship, etc.) in the first section of the lease.

Please also note that any forms which begin with "NOTICE" should be sent to the person or company receiving the form by certified U.S. mail. This may be a requirement under various laws.

In most cases, masculine and feminine terms have been eliminated and the generic "it" or "them" used instead. In the few situations in which this leads to awkward sentence construction, "his or her" or "he or she" may be used instead.

It is recommended that you review the table of contents of this book in order to gain a broad overview of the range and type of legal documents that are available. Then, before you prepare any of the forms for use, you should carefully read the introductory information and instructions in the chapter where the particular form is contained. Try to be as detailed and specific as possible as you fill in these forms. The more precise the description, the less likelihood that later disputes may develop over what was actually intended by the language chosen. The careful preparation and use of the legal forms in this book should provide the typical person with most of the landlord/tenant documents necessary for most common transactions relating to landlord/tenant situations. If in doubt as to whether a particular form will work in a specific application, please consult a competent lawyer.

Installation Instructions for the Forms-on-CD

Quick-Start Installation for PCs
1.   Insert the enclosed CD in your computer.
2.   The installation program will start automatically. Follow the onscreen dialogue and make your appropriate choices.
3.   If the CD installation does not start automatically, click on **START**, then **RUN**, then **BROWSE**, and select your CD drive, and then select the file "**Install.exe**." Finally, click OK to run the installation program.
4.   During the installation program, you will be prompted as to whether or not you wish to install the Adobe Acrobat Reader® program. If you do not already have the Adobe Acrobat Reader® program installed on your hard drive, you will need to select the full installation that will install this program to your computer.

Installation Instructions for MACs®
1.   Insert the enclosed CD in your computer.
2.   Copy the folder "**Forms for Macs**" to your hard drive. All of the PDF and text-only forms are included in this folder.
3.   If you do not already have the Adobe Acrobat Reader® program installed on your hard drive, you will need to download the version of this software that is appropriate for you particular MAC operating system from www.adobe.com. Note: The latest versions of the MAC operating system (OS-X) has PDF capabilities built into it.

Instructions for Using Forms-on-CD

All of the forms which are included in this book have been provided on the Forms-on-CD for your use if you have access to a computer. If you have completed the Forms-on-CD installation program, all of the forms will have been copied to your computer's hard drive. By default, these files are installed in the C:\Landlord Forms\Forms folder which is created by the installation program. (Note for MAC users: see instructions above). Opening the Forms folder will provide you with access to folders for each of the topics corresponding to chapters in the book. Within each chapter, the forms are provided in two separate formats:

Text forms which may opened, prepared, and printed from within your own word processing program (such as Microsoft Word®, or WordPerfect®). The text forms all have the file extension: .**txt**. These forms are located in the TEXT FORMS folders supplied for each chapter's forms. You may wish to use the forms in this format if you will be making changes to text of the forms. To access these forms, please see below.

PDF forms which may be filled in on your computer screen and printed out on any printer. This particular format provides the most widely-used cross-platform format for accessing computer files. Files in this format may be opened as images on your computer and printed out on any printer. The files in Adobe PDF format all have the file extension: .pdf. Although this format provides the easiest method for completing the forms, the forms in this format can not be altered (other than to fill in the information required on the blanks provided). To access the PDF forms, please see below. If you wish to alter the language in any of the forms, you will need to access the forms in their text-only versions. To access these text-only forms, please also see below.

To Access Adobe PDF Forms

1. You must have already installed the Adobe Acrobat Reader® program to your computer's hard drive. This program is installed automatically by the installation program. (MAC users will need to install this program via www.adobe.com).

2. On your computer's desktop, you will find a shortcut icon labeled "Acrobat Reader®" Using your mouse, left double click on this icon. This will open the Acrobat Reader® program. When the Acrobat Reader® program is opened for the first time, you will need to accept the Licensing Agreement from Adobe in order to use this program. Click "Accept" when given the option to accept or decline the Agreement.

3. Once the Acrobat Reader® program is open on your computer, click on FILE (in the upper left-hand corner of the upper taskbar). Then click on OPEN in the drop down menu. Depending on which version of Windows or other operating system you are using, a box will open which will allow you to access files on your computer's hard drive. The files for Landlord Forms are located on your computer's "C" drive, under the folder "Landlord Forms." In this folder, you will find a subfolder "Forms." (Note: if you installed the forms folder on a different drive, access the forms on that particular drive).

4. If you desire to work with one of the forms, you should then left double-click your mouse on the sub-folder: "Forms." This will open two folders: one for text forms and one for PDF forms. Left double click your mouse on the PDF forms folder and a list of the PDF forms for that topic should appear. Left double click your mouse on the form of your choice. This will open the appropriate form within the Adobe Acrobat Reader® program.

To Fill in Forms in the Adobe Acrobat Reader® Program

1. Once you have opened the appropriate form in the Acrobat Reader® program, filling in the form is a simple process. A 'hand tool' icon will be your cursor in the Acrobat Reader® program. Move the 'hand tool' cursor to the first blank space that will need to be completed on the form. A vertical line or "I-beam" should appear at the beginning of the first space on a form that you will need to fill in. You may then begin to type the necessary information in the space provided. When you have filled in the first blank

space, hit the **TAB** key on your keyboard. This will move the 'hand' cursor to the next space which must be filled in. Please note that some of the spaces in the forms must be completed by hand, specifically the signature blanks.

2. Move through the form, completing each required space, and hitting **TAB** to move to the next space to be filled in. For information on the information required for each blank on the forms, please read the instructions in this book. When you have completed all of the fill-ins, you may print out the form on your computer's printer. (Please note: hitting **TAB** after the last fill-in will return you to the first page of the form.)

3. IMPORTANT NOTE: Unfortunately, the Adobe Acrobat Reader® program does NOT allow you to save the filled-in form to your computer's hard drive. You can only save the form in a printed version. For this reason, you should wait to complete the forms until you have all of the information necessary to complete the chosen form in one session. You may, of course, leave the Acrobat program open on your computer and leave a partially-completed form open in the program. However, if you close the file or if you close the Acrobat Reader® program, the filled-in information will be lost.

To Access and Complete the Text Forms

For your convenience, all of the forms in this book are also provided as text-only forms which may be altered and saved. To open and use any of the text forms:

1. First, open your preferred word processing program. Then click on **FILE** (in the upper left-hand corner of the upper taskbar). Then click on **OPEN** in the drop down menu. Depending on which version of Windows or other operating system you are using, a box will open which will allow you to access files on your computer's hard drive. The files for Landlord Forms are located on your computer's "**C**" drive, under the folder "**Landlord Forms**." In this folder, you will find a sub-folder: "**Forms**."

2. If you desire to work with one of the forms, you should then left double-click your mouse on the sub-folder: "**Forms**." A list of form topics (corresponding to the chapters in the book) will appear and you should then left double-click your mouse on the topic of your choice. This will open two folders: one for text forms and one for PDF forms. Left double click your mouse on the text forms folder and a list of the text forms for that topic should appear. Left double click your mouse on the form of your choice. This will open the appropriate form within your word processing program.

3. You may now fill in the necessary information while the text-only file is open in your word processing program. You may need to adjust margins and/or line endings of the form to fit your particular word processing program. Note that there is an asterisk (*) in every location in these forms where information will need to be included. Replace each asterisk with the necessary information. When the form is complete, you may

print out the completed form and you may save the completed form. If you wish to save the completed form, you should rename the form so that your hard drive will retain an unaltered version of the form.

Technical Support

Nova Publishing will provide technical support for installing the provided software. Please also note that Nova Publishing Company cannot provide legal advice regarding the effect or use of the forms on this software. For questions about installing the Forms-on-CD, you may call Nova Technical Support at 1-800-748-1175.

In addition, Nova cannot provide technical support for the use of the Adobe Acrobat Reader®. For any questions relating to Adobe Acrobat Reader®, please access Adobe Technical Support at www.adobe.com/support/main.html or you may search for assistance in the HELP area of Adobe Acrobat Reader® (located in approximately the center of the top line of the program's desktop).

CHAPTER 2
Rental of Real Estate

A *lease* of real estate is simply a written contract for one party to rent a specific property from another for a certain amount and certain time period. As such, all of the general legal ramifications that relate to contracts also relate to leases. However, all states have additional requirements which pertain only to leases. If the rental period is to be for one year or more, all states require that leases be in writing. Leases can be prepared for *periodic tenancies* (that is, for example, month-to-month or week-to-week) or they can be for a fixed period. There are leases contained in this chapter that provide for both fixed-period tenancies and for month-to-month tenancies.

There are also general guidelines for security deposits in most states. These most often follow a reasonable pattern and should be adhered to. In general, most states provide for the following with regard to lease security deposits:

- Should be no greater than one month's rent and should be fully refundable
- Should be used for the repair of damages and/or cleaning of the property (beyond normal wear and tear) only, and not applied for the nonpayment of rent (an additional month's rent may be requested to cover potential nonpayment of rent situations)
- Should be kept in a separate, interest-bearing account and returned, with interest, to the tenant within 10 days of termination of a lease (minus, of course, any deductions for damages or cleaning)

Note that each state has its own requirements and they may vary substantially from the above general listing. You should refer to the Appendix of this book for the specific details regarding security deposits for your state.

In addition to state laws regarding security deposits, many states have requirements relating to the time periods required prior to terminating a lease. These rules have evolved over time to prevent both the landlord or the tenant from being harmed by early termination of a lease. In general, if the lease is for a fixed time period, the termination of the lease is governed by the lease itself. Early termination of a fixed-period lease may, however, be governed by individual state law. For periodic leases (month-to-month, etc.), there are normally state rules as to how much advance notice must be given prior to termination of a lease. If early lease termination is anticipated, check the state law in the Appendix of this book regarding this issue.

The Appendix of this book provides a state-by-state listing of the main provisions of landlord-tenant law for all 50 states and Washington D.C., including details of state laws regarding security deposits, entry into leased premises, and other rental issues. A few states require additional information in the lease relating to security deposits. Please see the Appendix for information on the requirements in your state. In addition, be advised that there may also be specific local laws that pertain to landlord and tenant relationships that may be applicable. You are advised to check any local ordinances or state laws for any possible additional requirements. Residents of California, Chicago, and Florida, please see below. You will also need to supply your tenant with a copy of the enclosed federal form: "Protect Your Family from Lead in Your Home," if the rental unit was built before 1978. Please also note that several states require the disclosure of various items to potential renters. The Appendix contains a listing of the residential real estate disclosure aspects of property law for each state. These disclosures, however, are generally intended for the sale of property, rather than rental. The Forms-on-CD provides several of the disclosure forms for California only. You may need to check for any local or state rental disclosure regulations that may apply in your situation.

In this chapter you will find a residential lease that covers most rental contingencies. Two commercial leases are also provided—a commercial gross lease under which a tenant pays a fixed rent and the landlord pays all of the upkeep on the property and all of the utilities (unless the utility is metered on the rented premises and the tenant agrees to pay) and a commercial net lease under which a tenant pays a fixed rent and additionally agrees to pay for all of the upkeep (maintenance, repairs, taxes, insurance, etc.) for the property and for all of the tenant's utility use. Additionally, there is a lease with purchase option for those situations where a tenant is given an option to purchase the property being rented and of having some or all of the rent applied to the purchase price. A final residential rental agreement is provided for those landlords and tenants who prefer to have the tenancy be on a month-to-month basis. This agreement is the month-to-month rental agreement.

For each of these rental agreements, a text version and a PDF format version are provided on the enclosed Forms-on-CD. If you are content with the form as it appears in this book, you may use the PDF version. However, if you would like to add or delete any text or clauses of any of these agreements, you will need to use the text version and make any changes in your word-processing program. Lease agreements for a few states will require the use of the text version in order to insert state-specific language into the lease. Please check the Appendix for details on your state.

Note to residents of California, Chicago, and Florida: A few additional required forms are provided in this chapter and on the Forms-on-CD for residents of these locales:

California Addendum to Lease
Chicago Addendum to Lease
Chicago Heating Disclosure Form (PDF form only, not fillable on a computer)
Chicago Residential Landlord and Tenant Ordinance Summary (PDF form not fillable)
Florida Attachment to Lease Regarding Security Deposits (Text form only)

Residential Lease: This form should be used when renting a residential property for a fixed period when you wish to include more detailed provisions. Although the landlord and tenant can agree to any terms they desire, this particular lease provides for the following basic terms to be included:

- A fixed-period term for the lease
- A security deposit for damages, cleaning or unpaid rent, which will be returned to tenant after the termination of the lease, with any charges deducted, but without interest unless required by state law
- A late payment fee and returned check penalty are agreed to
- That the tenant agrees to keep the property in good repair and not make any alterations without consent
- Tenant has inspected the property and has noted any unsafe, damaged, or unclean conditions
- Tenant agrees not to conduct any business or store any dangerous material on the property and agrees to notify landlord of any problems with the property
- Tenant agrees to use the property only as a single family residence and only with a noted number of tenants
- Tenant agrees to comply with all applicable laws and regulations
- Tenant agrees not to have any pets without permission of the landlord
- That landlord and tenant agree on who will pay utilities
- That the tenant agrees not to assign the lease or sublet the property without the landlord's consent
- That the landlord has the right to inspect the property on a reasonable basis,
- That the landlord has the right to re-enter and take possession upon breach of the lease (as long as it is in accordance with state law)
- Once the lease term has expired, any continued occupancy will be as a month-to month tenancy
- Landlord makes a required statement regarding radon gas
- Landlord discloses information regarding lead paint and tenant acknowledges receipt of this information and the following pamphlet
- That the landlord will provide tenant with the U.S. EPA lead pamphlet: "Protect Your Family from Lead in Your Home." *Note*: This document is provided on the Forms-on-CD and is necessary *only* if the rental dwelling was built prior to 1978
- Any other additional terms that the parties agree upon
- That any required notices must be sent to the landlord's and tenant's addresses as noted in the lease itself
- Finally, this lease notes that the landlord and tenant agree that the lease is the entire agreement and that it binds both landlord and tenant and any successors to the lease, that if there is any lawsuit to enforce the lease, whoever wins will pay the other parties legal fees and costs, and that the lease is governed by the laws of a particular state.

Note: You will also need to supply your tenant with a copy of the federal form: "Protect Your Family from Lead in Your Home" if the property was built prior to 1978. This form is included in Chapter 5 and on the Forms-on-CD. (Note: Residents of California will need to include the California Addendum to Lease form. Residents of Chicago will need to include the Chicago Addendum to Lease and other required Chicago forms. Residents of Florida will need to included the Florida Attachment to Lease Regarding Security Deposits. These forms are included in this chapter and on the Forms-on-CD). Residents of Florida, Maryland, and Michigan will need to add additional language to the lease form and must use the text formatted version of this lease on the Forms-on-CD in order to do so. Residents of all states should check the Appendix for any applicable provisions of their own state's laws.

If you wish to alter any of the terms of this lease or add additional terms, you will need to use the text formatted version of this lease on the Forms-on-CD. To prepare this form, fill in the following information:

① Date of lease
② Name and address of landlord
③ Name and address of tenant
④ Complete address of leased property
⑤ Beginning date of lease
⑥ End date of lease
⑦ Amount of the rental payment
⑧ Length of period (usually, month)
⑨ Day of the period when rent will be due
⑩ Due date of first rental payment
⑪ Amount of daily late charge (Note: some states restrict this amount–See Appendix)
⑫ State in which property is located
⑬ Amount of charge for returned check
⑭ Amount of security deposit for damages, cleaning or unpaid rent (Check Appendix)
⑮ Number of days to return deposit to tenant after end of lease (Check Appendix)
⑯ State in which property is located
⑰ If required: name, address, and possibly account # for holding deposit (Check Appendix)
⑱ Tenant's list of problems with property (based on pre-lease inspection)
⑲ Maximum number of tenants
⑳ State in which property is located
㉑ Utilities that landlord will supply
㉒ Utilities that tenant will provide
㉓ State in which property is located
㉔ State in which property is located
㉕ Landlord's initials on presence of lead paint disclosure
㉖ Landlord's initials on records and/or reports of lead paint
㉗ Tenant's initials on lead paint acknowledgment
㉘ Any other additional terms
㉙ Which state's laws will be used to interpret lease
㉚ Signature of landlord
㉛ Printed name of landlord
㉜ Signature of tenant
㉝ Printed name of tenant

Residential Lease

The following lease is entered into on this date: ①_____, by and
between ②_____ , landlord,
address: ②

and ③_____ , tenant,
address: ③

1. The landlord agrees to rent to the tenant and the tenant agrees to rent from the landlord
   the following residence: ④

2. The term of this lease will be from ⑤_____ , 20 ⑤___ , until
   _____ , 20 ⑥___ .

3. The rental payments will be $ ⑦_____ per ⑧_____ and will
   be payable by the tenant to the landlord on the ⑨_____ day of each month,
   beginning on ⑩_____ , 20 ⑩___ .

4. If the rental payment is late, the tenant agrees to pay an additional charge of $ ⑪_____
   per day as late rent penalty, except as limited by the laws of the State of ⑫_____ .

5. If any check offered by the tenant is returned for insufficient funds, the tenant agrees to
   pay the landlord a returned check charge of $ ⑬_____ .

6. The tenant has paid the landlord a security deposit of $ ⑭_____ . This
   security deposit will be held as security for a). the repair of any damages to the residence
   by the tenant beyond normal wear and tear and/or b). cleaning the residence to the condition property was in upon moving in and/or c). non-payment of rent. This deposit will
   be returned to the tenant within ⑮_____ days of the termination of this lease,
   minus any amounts needed to repair or clean the residence or for unpaid rent, but without
   interest, except as required by law in the State of ⑯_____ .

Tenant agrees that if any damages to the property (caused by tenant or tenant's guests misuse or neglect of the property) are greater than this security deposit, then tenant shall pay for any additional damages. This deposit may NOT be applied by tenant to the tenant's last month's rent. If required by law, the security deposit will be held in the following account: ⑰ _____

_____ .

7. Tenant agrees to maintain the residence in a clean and sanitary manner and not to make any alterations to the residence without the landlord's written consent, except as required by law. At the termination of this lease, the tenant agrees to leave the residence in the same condition as when it was received, except for normal wear and tear.

8. Tenant has inspected the premises and found them to be in good, safe and clean condition, unless noted here: ⑱

9. Tenant also agrees not to conduct any type of business in the residence, nor store or use any dangerous or hazardous materials. Tenant agrees that the landlord will be notified immediately of any damages, defects, or dangerous conditions regarding the property.

10. Tenant agrees that the residence is to be used only as a single family residence, with a maximum of   ⑲ _____ tenants.

11. Tenant also agrees to comply with all rules, laws, and ordinances affecting the residence, including all laws of the State of ⑳ _____ .

12. Tenant agrees that no pets or other animals are allowed in the residence without the written permission of the Landlord.

13. The landlord agrees to supply the following utilities to the tenant: ㉑

14. The tenant agrees to obtain and pay for the following utilities: ㉒

15. Tenant agrees not to sublet the residence or assign this lease without the landlord's written consent.

16. Tenant agrees to allow the landlord reasonable access to the residence for inspection and repair. Landlord agrees to enter the residence only after notifying the tenant in advance, except in an emergency, and according to the laws of the State of ㉓_____.

17. If the tenant fails to pay the rent on time or violates any other terms of this lease, the landlord will have the right to terminate this lease in accordance with state law. The landlord will also have the right to re-enter the residence and take possession of it and to take advantage of any other legal remedies available under the laws of the State of ㉔_____.

18. If the Tenant remains as tenant after the expiration of this lease without signing a new lease, a month-to-month tenancy will be created with the same terms and conditions as this lease, except that such new tenancy may be terminated by thirty (30) days written notice from either the Tenant or the Landlord.

19. As required by law, the landlord makes the following statement: "Radon gas is a naturally occurring radioactive gas that, when accumulated in sufficient quantities in a building, may present health risks to persons exposed to it. Levels of radon gas that exceed federal and state guidelines have been found in buildings in this state. Additional information regarding radon gas and radon gas testing may be obtained from your county health department."

20. As required by law, the landlord makes the following **LEAD WARNING STATEMENT**:

"Every purchaser or lessee of any interest in residential real property on which a residential dwelling was built prior to 1978 is notified that such property may present exposure to lead from lead-based paint that may place young children at risk of developing lead poisoning. Lead poisoning in young children may produce permanent neurological damage, including learning disabilities, reduced intelligence quotient, behavioral problems, and impaired memory. Lead poisoning also poses a particular threat to pregnant women. The seller or lessor of any interest in residential real estate is required to provide the buyer with any information on lead-based paint hazards from risk assessments or inspection in the seller's or lessor's possession and notify the buyer or lessee of any known lead-based paint hazards. A risk assessment or inspection for possible lead-based paint hazards is recommended prior to purchase."

Landlord's Disclosure

Presence of lead-based paint and/or lead-based paint hazards: (Landlord to initial one).

㉕_____ Known lead-based paint and/or lead-based paint hazards are present in building (explain):

㉕_____ Landlord has no knowledge of lead-based paint and/or lead-based paint hazards in building.

Records and reports available to landlord: (Landlord to initial one).

___(26)___ Landlord has provided tenant with all available records and reports pertaining to lead-based paint and/or lead-based paint hazards are present in building (list documents):

___(26)___ Landlord has no records and reports pertaining to lead-based paint and/or lead-based paint hazards in building.

Tenant's Acknowledgment

(Tenant to initial all applicable).

___(27)___ Tenant has received copies of all information listed above.

___(27)___ Tenant has received the pamphlet "Protect Your Family from Lead in Your Home."

___(27)___ Tenant has received a ten (10)-day opportunity (or mutually agreed on period) to conduct a risk assessment or inspection for the presence of lead-based paint and/or lead-based paint hazards in building.

___(27)___ Tenant has waived the opportunity to conduct a risk assessment or inspection for the presence of lead-based paint and/or lead-based paint hazards in building.

The landlord and tenant have reviewed the information above and certify, by their signatures at the end of this lease, to the best of their knowledge, that the information they have provided is true and accurate.

21. The following are additional terms of this lease: (28)

22. The parties agree that this lease is the entire agreement between them.

23. Any required notices must be sent to the landlord's and tenant's addresses first noted to be valid.

24. This lease binds and benefits both the landlord and tenant and any successors.

25. In any legal proceeding to enforce any part of this lease, the prevailing party shall recover reasonable court costs and attorney's fees.

26. This lease is governed by the laws of the State of ㉙ _____ .

㉚ _____

Signature of Landlord

㉜ _____

Signature of Tenant

㉛ _____

Printed Name of Landlord

㉝ _____

Printed Name of Tenant

Commercial Gross Lease: This form should be used when renting a commercial property in those situations when the tenant pays a fixed rental payment and the landlord pays for upkeep, repairs, overhead and utilities for the property. (Note: if a utility is metered separately and located within the leased area, it may be more practical for the tenant to pay that particular utility. If this is the situation, simply include a brief paragraph to that effect at the end of the lease, under the paragraph for additional terms.) Although the landlord and tenant can agree to any terms they desire, this particular lease provides for the following basic terms to be included:

- A clear description of the property leased and regarding what the lease includes (such as parking facilities, restroom access, storage areas, and access to common areas of a building—such as stairs, elevators, and halls)
- An initial fixed-period term for the lease, with the having an option to renew the lease with a 90-day notice to the landlord
- Any renewal of the lease is subject to a rent increase based on a ratio of the property taxes current when the lease begins and the property taxes when the lease is renewed. The initial property taxes will be the denominator of the ratio and the renewal date property taxes will be the numerator of the ratio.
  Here is an example: Property is leased for $1,000.00 per month and the property taxes are $5,000.00 at the beginning of the lease. If property taxes increase to $6,000.00 at the time for the lease renewal, the ratio is 6000/5000 or 1.2. Thus, the rent would be increased to $1,200.00 (or $1,000.00 X 1.2)
- A late charge for rent payments
- A fee for any returned checks
- A limitation on what business the tenant may conduct on the property
- A security deposit for damages, cleaning or unpaid rent, which will be returned to tenant after the termination of the lease, with any charges deducted, but without interest unless required by state law
- The tenant agrees to conduct only a specified business on the premises
- The tenant agrees to install only specified equipment on the premises and be responsible for their upkeep, maintenance, and removal
- The tenant has inspected the premises and found it in satisfactory condition
- The landlord represents that the property is properly zoned and is in compliance with all applicable laws and regulations
- That the landlord is responsible for the upkeep of the exterior and the upkeep of the interior of the property, other than the tenant's installed equipment and the cleaning and maintenance of the interior of the leased property
- That the tenant agrees to keep the property in good repair and not make any alterations without consent
- The landlord is responsible for real estate taxes and the tenant is responsible for any personal property taxes for tenant's property
- Tenant agrees to leave the property in good condition at the end of the lease

- Tenant agrees to comply with all applicable laws and regulations
- Landlord agrees to pay for all utilities, unless otherwise noted in lease
- That the tenant agrees not to assign the lease or sublet the property without the landlord's consent
- That the landlord has the right to inspect the property on a reasonable basis, and that the tenant has already inspected it and found it satisfactory
- That the landlord has the right to re-enter and take possession upon breach of the lease (as long as it is in accordance with state law)
- That the landlord will carry fire and casualty insurance on the property, and that the tenant will carry casualty insurance on their own equipment and fixtures and also carry general business liability insurance
- If the property is damaged and it is not the tenant's fault and the tenant is deprived of occupancy, the tenant need not pay rent. If the loss of occupancy lasts more than 90 days, the tenant may terminate the lease by delivering a notice of termination to the landlord
- That the lease is subject to any mortgage or deed of trust and that the tenant agrees to sign any future subordination documents
- Otherwise, the lease may only be terminated by notice or a violation of the lease
- The landlord supplies a radon gas statement
- Any other additional terms that the parties agree upon
- Any attachments that the parties agree upon
- That any disputes will be settled by a mutually selected mediator whose fee will be paid split equally among the landlord and tenant
- That any required notices must be sent to the landlord's and tenant's addresses as noted in the lease itself
- That the lease is the entire agreement and is intended to comply with all laws, binds and benefits both parties and their successors, and is governed by the laws of the state upon which they both agree.

Residents of all states should check the Appendix for any applicable provisions of their own state's laws.

If you wish to alter any of the terms of this lease or add additional terms, you will need to use the text formatted version of this lease on the Forms-on-CD.

To prepare this form, fill in the following information:

① Date of lease
② Complete name and address of landlord
③ Complete name and address of tenant
④ Complete address and description of leased property

⑤ Complete description of any additional inclusions in the lease (such as parking facilities, restroom access, storage areas, and access to common areas of a building—such as stairs, elevators, and halls.)

⑥ Beginning date of lease

⑦ End date of lease

⑧ Amount of rental payment and length of period (usually, month, but may be annually and based on a square footage amount)

⑨ Day of the period when rent will be due and length of period (usually, month, but may be annually)

⑩ Due date of first rent payment

⑪ Amount of late rent penalty

⑫ State in which property is located

⑬ Amount of returned check charge

⑭ Amount of security deposit for damages, cleaning or unpaid rent

⑮ Number of days after termination when deposit is due tenant

⑯ State in which property is located

⑰ Description of tenant's business

⑱ Description of any equipment and fixtures to be installed by tenant

⑲ Number of days allowed tenant to correct any defaults or violations of lease

⑳ Number of days notice required to tenant for landlord to terminate lease for any defaults or violations of lease

㉑ Minimum amount of business liability insurance tenant will carry per occurrence

㉒ Minimum amount of business liability insurance tenant will carry per year

㉓ Number of days required for termination of lease for other than violation or default

㉔ Any other additional terms

㉕ Any attachments to lease

㉖ Which state's laws will be used to interpret lease

㉗ Signature of landlord

㉘ Printed name of landlord

㉙ Signature of tenant

㉚ Printed name of tenant

Commercial Gross Lease

The following lease is entered into on this date: ___(1)_____, by and
between ___(2)_____ , landlord,
address: ___(2)___

and ___(3)_____ , tenant,
address: ___(3)___

1. The landlord agrees to rent to the tenant and the tenant agrees to rent from the landlord the following commercial property: (4)

2. Tenant's use of the leased property includes the following: (5)

3. The term of this lease will be from ___(6)_____ , 20 (6)___ , until
   ___(7)_____ , 20 (7)___ .

4. The rental payments will be $ ___(8)_____ per ___(8)_____ and will be payable by the tenant to the landlord on the ___(9)_____ day of each month, beginning on ___(10)_____ , 20 (10)___ .

5. If the tenant has not violated any terms of this lease, the tenant shall have an option to renew this lease which must be exercised in writing 90 days in advance of the termination

of this lease. Any such renewal will be subject to the same terms and conditions as this lease, including the possible rental increase contemplated by the following paragraph.

6. The base rental payments may be increased on an annual basis proportionately based on any increase in the property taxes for the leased property for the prior year. The latest assessed property taxes for the property when first occupied shall be the denominator for any proportionate rent increases and the latest assessed property taxes at the time of the anniversary of the lease shall be the numerator for any proportionate rent increases.

7. If the rental payment is late, the tenant agrees to pay an additional charge of $ ⑪_____ per day as late rent penalty, except as limited by the laws of the State of ⑫_____.

8. If any check offered by the tenant is returned for insufficient funds, the tenant agrees to pay the landlord a returned check charge of $ ⑬_____.

9. The tenant has paid the landlord a security deposit of $ ⑭_____. This security deposit will be held as security for a). the repair of any damages to the property by the tenant beyond normal wear and tear and/or b). cleaning the property to the condition property was in upon moving in and/or c). non-payment of rent. This deposit will be returned to the tenant within ⑮_____ days of the termination of this lease, minus any amounts needed to repair or clean the property or for unpaid rent, but without interest, except as required by law in the State of ⑯_____. tenant agrees that if any damages to the property (caused by tenant or tenant's employees or agents misuse or neglect of the property) are greater than this security deposit, then tenant shall pay for any additional damages. This deposit may NOT be applied by tenant to the tenant's last month's rent.

10. The tenant agrees to use the property only for the purpose of carrying on the following lawful business: ⑰

11. The landlord agrees that the tenant may install only the following equipment and fixtures for the purpose of operating the tenant's business and that such equipment and fixtures shall remain the property of the tenant and that the tenant shall be solely responsible for their maintenance and upkeep and for their timely and orderly removal at the termination of this lease: ⑱

12. The tenant has inspected the property and has found it satisfactory for its intended purposes.

13. The landlord represents that the property is properly zoned for the tenant's stated purpose and that, at the time this lease is entered into, is in compliance with all applicable laws, ordinances and regulations.

14. The landlord shall be responsible for the repair, cleaning, maintenance, and upkeep of the exterior of the property, including the exterior common areas, roof, exterior walls, parking areas, landscaping, and building foundation. The landlord shall also be responsible for the repair and upkeep of the interior of the property, including interior common areas, all electrical, mechanical, plumbing, heating, cooling, or any other system or equipment on the property, except any property installed by tenant under the terms of this lease. Tenant shall be responsible for the maintenance of the interior of the leased property in a clean, safe and sanitary manner.

15. The landlord shall be responsible for any real property taxes for the leased property. Tenant shall be responsible for any personal property taxes assessed against its personal property that is present on the leased property.

16. Tenant agrees not to make any alterations to the property without the landlord's written consent.

17. At the termination of this Lease, the tenant agrees to leave the property in the same condition as when it was received, except for normal wear and tear.

18. Tenant also agrees to comply with all rules, laws, regulations, and ordinances affecting the property or the business activities of the tenant.

19. The landlord agrees to obtain and pay for all necessary utilities for the property, unless otherwise noted in this lease.

20. The tenant agrees not to sub-let the property or assign this Lease without the landlord's written consent, which shall not be unreasonably withheld.

21. Tenant agrees to allow the landlord reasonable access to the property for inspection and repair. Landlord agrees to enter the property only after notifying the tenant in advance, except in an emergency.

22. If the tenant fails to pay the rent on time or violates any other terms of this Lease, the landlord will provide written notice of the violation or default, allowing ⑲ _____ days to correct the violation or default. If the violation or default is not completely corrected within the time prescribed, the landlord will have the right to terminate this Lease with ⑳ _____ days notice and in accordance with state law. Upon termination of this Lease, the tenant agrees to surrender possession of the property. The landlord will also have the right to re-enter the property and take possession of it, remove tenant

and any equipment or possessions of tenant, and to take advantage of any other legal remedies available.

23. The landlord agrees to carry fire and casualty insurance on the property, but shall have no liability for the operation of the tenant's business. The tenant agrees not to do anything that will increase the landlord's insurance premiums and, further agrees to indemnify and hold the landlord harmless from any liability, loss, injury, or damage, whether caused by tenant's operations or otherwise.

24. The tenant agrees to carry and pay all premiums for casualty insurance on any equipment or fixtures that tenant installs at the property. In addition, the tenant agrees to carry business liability insurance, including bodily injury and property damage coverage, covering all tenant's business operations in the amount of $ ㉑_____ per occurrence and $ ㉒_____ per year, with the landlord named as a co-insured party. tenant agrees to furnish landlord copies of the insurance policies and to not cancel the policies without notifying the landlord in advance. Tenant agrees to provide landlord with a Certificate of Insurance which indicates that landlord is a co-insured party and that landlord shall be provided with a minimum of ten (10) days written notice prior to cancellation or change of coverage.

25. If the property is damaged through fire or any other cause that is not the fault of the tenant, tenant shall owe no rent for any period during which tenant is deprived of occupancy of the property. If the tenant is deprived of occupancy for over 90 days, tenant shall have the option of terminating this lease by delivering a written notice of termination to the landlord at the address for the landlord first noted in this lease.

26. This Lease is subject to any mortgage or deed of trust currently on the property or which may be made against the property at any time in the future. The tenant agrees to sign any documents necessary to subordinate this Lease to a mortgage or deed of trust for the landlord.

27. This Lease may only be terminated by ㉓_____ days written notice from either party, except in the event of a violation of any terms or default of any payments or responsibilities due under this Lease, which are governed by the terms in Paragraph 22 of this Lease.

28. Tenant agrees that if any legal action is necessary to recover the property, collect any amounts due under this Lease, or correct a violation of any term of this Lease, tenant shall be responsible for all costs incurred by landlord in connection with such action, including any reasonable attorney's fees.

29. As required by law, the landlord makes the following statement: "Radon gas is a naturally-occurring radioactive gas that, when accumulated in sufficient quantities in a building, may present health risks to persons exposed to it. Levels of radon gas that exceed federal and state guidelines have been found in buildings in this state. Additional information regarding radon gas and radon gas testing may be obtained from your county health department."

30. The following are additional terms of this Lease: ㉔

31. The parties agree that the following attachments are part of this lease and are incorporated by reference: ㉕

32. The parties agree that any disputes under this lease will be conducted by a mediator mutually selected by the parties and that the parties will share the cost of such mediation equally. Landlord need not, however, participate in any mediation unless tenant has paid all rent due or placed the rent due in escrow with the agreed-upon mediator.

33. The parties agree that is the entire agreement between them and that no terms of this Lease may be changed except by written agreement of both parties. Any required notices must be sent to the landlord's and tenant's addresses first noted to be valid.

34. This Lease is intended to comply with any and all applicable laws relating to landlord and tenant relationships in this state.

35. This Lease binds and benefits both the landlord and tenant and any heirs, successors, representatives, or assigns.

36. This Lease is governed by the laws of the State of ㉖______ .

㉗______________________________
Signature of Landlord

㉘______________________________
Printed Name of Landlord

㉙______________________________
Signature of Tenant

㉚______________________________
Printed Name of Tenant

Commercial Net Lease: This form should be used when renting a commercial property when the tenant will be responsible for some or, perhaps , all of the property's repairs, maintenance, and insurance. Although the landlord and tenant can agree to any terms they desire, this particular lease provides for the following basic terms to be included:

- A clear description of the property leased and regarding what the lease includes (such as parking facilities, restroom access, storage areas, and access to common areas of a building—such as stairs, elevators, and halls)
- An initial fixed-period term for the lease, with the having an option to renew the lease with a 90-day notice to the landlord
- Any renewal of the lease is subject to a rent increase based on a ratio of the property taxes current when the lease begins and the property taxes when the lease is renewed. The initial property taxes will be the denominator of the ratio and the renewal date property taxes will be the numerator of the ratio.
  Here is an example: Property is leased for $1,000.00 per month and the property taxes are $5,000.00 at the beginning of the lease. If property taxes increase to $6,000.00 at the time for the lease renewal, the ratio is 6000/5000 or 1.2. Thus, the rent would be increased to $1,200.00 (or $1,000.00 X 1.2)
- A late charge for rent payments
- A fee for any returned checks
- A limitation on what business the tenant may conduct on the property
- A security deposit for damages, cleaning or unpaid rent, which will be returned to tenant after the termination of the lease, with any charges deducted, but without interest unless required by state law
- The tenant agrees to conduct only a specified business on the premises
- The tenant agrees to install only specified equipment on the premises and be responsible for their upkeep, maintenance, and removal
- The tenant has inspected the premises and found it in satisfactory condition
- The landlord represents that the property is properly zoned and is in compliance with all applicable laws and regulations
- That the tenant is responsible for the upkeep, cleaning, and maintenance of the exterior and interior of the property
- That the tenant agrees to keep the property in good repair and not make any alterations without consent
- The landlord is responsible for real estate taxes and the tenant for any personal property taxes for the property
- Tenant agrees to leave the property in good condition at the end of the lease
- Tenant agrees to comply with all applicable laws and regulations
- Tenant agrees to pay for all utilities, unless otherwise noted in lease
- That the tenant agrees not to assign the lease or sublet the property without the landlord's consent

- That the landlord has the right to inspect the property on a reasonable basis, and that the tenant has already inspected it and found it satisfactory
- That the landlord has the right to re-enter and take possession upon breach of the lease (as long as it is in accordance with state law)
- That the tenant will carry fire and casualty insurance on the property, and that the tenant will carry casualty insurance on their own equipment and fixtures and also carry general business liability insurance
- That the lease is subject to any mortgage or deed of trust and that the tenant agrees to sign any future subordination documents
- The lease may only be terminated by notice or a violation of the lease or for other cause with sufficient notice
- The landlord supplies a radon gas statement
- Any other additional terms that the parties agree upon
- Any attachments that the parties agree upon
- That any disputes will be settled by a mutually selected mediator whose fee will be paid split equally among the landlord and tenant
- That any required notices must be sent to the landlord's and tenant's addresses as noted in the lease itself
- That the lease is the entire agreement and is intended to comply with all laws, binds and benefits both parties and their successors, and is governed by the laws of the state upon which they both agree.

Residents of all states should check the Appendix for any applicable provisions of their own state's laws.

If you wish to alter any of the terms of this lease or add additional terms, you will need to use the text formatted version of this lease on the Forms-on-CD.

To prepare this form, fill in the following information:

1. Date of lease
2. Complete name and address of landlord
3. Complete name and address of tenant
4. Complete address and description of leased property
5. Complete description of any additional inclusions in the lease (such as parking facilities, restroom access, storage areas, and access to common areas of a building—such as stairs, elevators, and halls.)
6. Beginning date of lease
7. End date of lease
8. Amount of rental payment and length of period (usually, month, but may be annually and based on a square footage amount)
9. Day of the period when rent will be due.
10. Due date of first rent payment

⑪ Amount of late rent penalty

⑫ State in which property is located

⑬ Amount of returned check charge

⑭ Amount of security deposit for damages, cleaning or unpaid rent

⑮ Number of days after termination when deposit is due tenant

⑯ State in which property is located

⑰ Description of tenant's business

⑱ Description of any equipment and fixtures to be installed by tenant

⑲ Number of days allowed tenant to correct any defaults or violations of lease

⑳ Number of days notice required to tenant for landlord to terminate lease for any defaults or violations of lease

㉑ Minimum amount of fire and casualty insurance tenant will carry

㉒ Minimum amount of business liability insurance tenant will carry per occurrence

㉓ Minimum amount of business liability insurance tenant will carry per year

㉔ Number of days required for termination of lease for other than violation or default

㉕ Any other additional terms

㉖ Any attachments to lease

㉗ Which state's laws will be used to interpret lease

㉘ Signature of landlord

㉙ Printed name of landlord

㉚ Signature of tenant

㉛ Printed name of tenant

Commercial Net Lease

The following lease is entered into on this date: ① _____, by and between ② _____, landlord,
address: ②

and ③ _____, tenant,
address: ③

1. The landlord agrees to rent to the tenant and the tenant agrees to rent from the landlord the following commercial property: ④

2. Tenant's use of the leased property includes the following: ⑤

3. The term of this lease will be from ⑥ _____, 20 ⑥ ____, until
   ⑦ _____, 20 ⑦ ____.

4. The rental payments will be $ ⑧ _____ per ⑧ _____ and will be payable by the tenant to the landlord on the ⑨ _____ day of each month, beginning on ⑩ _____, 20 ⑩ ____.

5. If the tenant has not violated any terms of this lease, the tenant shall have an option to renew this lease which must be exercised in writing 90 days in advance of the termination

of this lease. Any such renewal will be subject to the same terms and conditions as this lease, including the possible rental increase contemplated by the following paragraph.

6. The base rental payments may be increased on an annual basis proportionately based on any increase in the property taxes for the leased property for the prior year. The latest assessed property taxes for the property when first occupied shall be the denominator for any proportionate rent increase ratio and the latest assessed property taxes at the time of the anniversary of the lease shall be the numerator for any proportionate rent increase ratio.

7. If the rental payment is late, the tenant agrees to pay an additional charge of $ ⑪ _____ per day as late rent penalty, except as limited by the laws of the State of ⑫ _____.

8. If any check offered by the tenant is returned for insufficient funds, the tenant agrees to pay the landlord a returned check charge of $ ⑬ _____.

9. The tenant has paid the landlord a security deposit of $ ⑭ _____. This security deposit will be held as security for a). the repair of any damages to the property by the tenant beyond normal wear and tear and/or b). cleaning the property to the condition property was in upon moving in and/or c). non-payment of rent. This deposit will be returned to the tenant within ⑮ _____ days of the termination of this lease, minus any amounts needed to repair or clean the property or for unpaid rent, but without interest, except as required by law in the State of ⑯ _____. Tenant agrees that if any damages to the property (caused by tenant or tenant's employees or agents misuse or neglect of the property) are greater than this security deposit, then tenant shall pay for any additional damages. This deposit may NOT be applied by tenant to the tenant's last month's rent.

10. The tenant agrees to use the property only for the purpose of carrying on the following lawful business: ⑰

11. The landlord agrees that the tenant may install only the following equipment and fixtures for the purpose of operating the tenant's business and that such equipment and fixtures shall remain the property of the tenant and that the tenant shall be solely responsible for their maintenance and upkeep and for their timely and orderly removal at the termination of this lease: ⑱

12. The tenant has inspected the property and has found it satisfactory for its intended purposes.

13. The landlord represents that the property is properly zoned for the tenant's stated purpose and that, at the time this lease is entered into, is in compliance with all applicable laws, ordinances and regulations.

14. The tenant shall be responsible for the repair, cleaning, maintenance, and upkeep of the exterior of the property, including the exterior common areas, roof, exterior walls, parking areas, landscaping, and building foundation. The tenant shall also be responsible for the repair, cleaning, maintenance, and upkeep of the interior of the property, including interior common areas, all electrical, mechanical, plumbing, heating, cooling, or any other system or equipment on the property. Tenant shall be responsible for the maintenance of the interior and exterior of the leased property in a clean, safe and sanitary manner.

15. The landlord shall be responsible for any real property taxes for the leased property. Tenant shall be responsible for any personal property taxes assessed against its personal property that is present on the leased property.

16. Tenant agrees not to make any alterations to the property without the landlord's written consent.

17. At the termination of this Lease, the tenant agrees to leave the property in the same condition as when it was received, except for normal wear and tear.

18. Tenant also agrees to comply with all rules, laws, regulations, and ordinances affecting the property or the business activities of the tenant.

19. The tenant agrees to obtain and pay for all necessary utilities for the property, unless otherwise noted in this lease.

20. The tenant agrees not to sub-let the property or assign this Lease without the landlord's written consent, which shall not be unreasonably withheld.

21. Tenant agrees to allow the landlord reasonable access to the property for inspection. Landlord agrees to enter the property only after notifying the tenant in advance, except in an emergency.

22. If the tenant fails to pay the rent on time or violates any other terms of this Lease, the landlord will provide written notice of the violation or default, allowing ⑲＿＿＿＿ days to correct the violation or default. If the violation or default is not completely corrected within the time prescribed, the landlord will have the right to terminate this Lease with ⑳＿＿＿＿ days notice and in accordance with state law. Upon termination of this Lease, the tenant agrees to surrender possession of the property. The landlord will also have the right to re-enter the property and take possession of it, remove tenant and any equipment or possessions of tenant, and to take advantage of any other legal remedies available.

23. The tenant agrees to carry fire and casualty insurance on the property in the amount of $ ㉑_____ . The tenant agrees to indemnify and hold the landlord harmless from any liability, loss, injury, or damage, whether caused by tenant's operations or otherwise.

24. The tenant agrees to carry and pay all premiums for casualty insurance on any equipment or fixtures that tenant installs at the property. In addition, the tenant agrees to carry business liability insurance, including bodily injury and property damage coverage, covering all tenant's business operations in the amount of $ ㉒_____ per occurrence and $ ㉓_____ per year, with the landlord named as a co-insured party. Tenant agrees to furnish landlord copies of the insurance policies and to not cancel the policies without notifying the landlord in advance. Tenant agrees to provide landlord with a Certificate of Insurance which indicates that landlord is a co-insured party and that landlord shall be provided with a minimum of ten (10) days written notice prior to cancellation or change of coverage.

25. If the property is damaged through fire or any other cause that is not the fault of the tenant, tenant shall owe no rent for any period during which tenant is deprived of occupancy of the property. If the tenant is deprived of occupancy for over 90 days, tenant shall have the option of terminating this lease by delivering a written notice of termination to the landlord at the address for the landlord first noted in this lease.

26. This Lease is subject to any mortgage or deed of trust currently on the property or which may be made against the property at any time in the future. The tenant agrees to sign any documents necessary to subordinate this Lease to a mortgage or deed of trust for the landlord.

27. This Lease may only be terminated by ㉔_____ days written notice from either party, except in the event of a violation of any terms or default of any payments or responsibilities due under this Lease, which are governed by the terms in Paragraph 22 of this Lease.

28. Tenant agrees that if any legal action is necessary to recover the property, collect any amounts due under this Lease, or correct a violation of any term of this Lease, tenant shall be responsible for all costs incurred by landlord in connection with such action, including any reasonable attorney's fees.

29. As required by law, the landlord makes the following statement: "Radon gas is a naturally-occurring radioactive gas that, when accumulated in sufficient quantities in a building, may present health risks to persons exposed to it. Levels of radon gas that exceed federal and state guidelines have been found in buildings in this state. Additional information regarding radon gas and radon gas testing may be obtained from your county health department."

30. The following are additional terms of this Lease: ㉕

31. The parties agree that the following attachments are part of this lease and are incorporated by reference: ㉖

32. The parties agree that any disputes under this lease will be conducted by a mediator mutually selected by the parties and that the parties will share the cost of such mediation equally. Landlord need not, however, participate in any mediation unless tenant has paid all rent due or placed the rent due in escrow with the agreed-upon mediator.

33. The parties agree that is the entire agreement between them and that no terms of this Lease may be changed except by written agreement of both parties. Any required notices must be sent to the landlord's and tenant's addresses first noted to be valid.

34. This Lease is intended to comply with any and all applicable laws relating to landlord and tenant relationships in this state.

35. This Lease binds and benefits both the landlord and tenant and any heirs, successors, representatives, or assigns.

36. This Lease is governed by the laws of the State of ㉗_____ .

㉘ _____
Signature of Landlord

㉙ _____
Printed Name of Landlord

㉚ _____
Signature of Tenant

㉛ _____
Printed Name of Tenant

Lease with Purchase Option: This lease provides for a fixed-period tenancy and contains a "purchase option" which offers the tenant a time period in which to have an exclusive option to purchase a parcel of real estate. Through the use of this agreement, the landlord can offer the tenant a time period with which to consider the purchase without concern of a sale to another party. This option provides that in exchange for a percentage of the rent (which will be applied to the purchase price if the option is exercised), the tenant is given a period of time to exercise the option and accept the terms of a completed real estate contract. If the tenant accepts the terms and exercises the option in writing, the landlord agrees to complete the sale. If the option is not exercised, the landlord is then free to sell the property on the market and retain the money paid for the option as rent. Although the landlord and tenant can agree to any terms they desire, this particular lease provides for the following basic terms to be included:

- A fixed-period term for the lease
- Tenant is given an option to purchase the leased property for a fixed period. If tenant exercises the option, landlord and tenant agree to enter into a standard Real Estate Sales Contract based on the terms laid out in this lease with option.
- A percentage (up to 100%) of the rent may be applied to the purchase price
- A late payment fee is agreed to
- A returned check fee is agreed to
- A security deposit for damages, cleaning or unpaid rent, which will be returned to tenant after the termination of the lease, with any charges deducted, but without interest unless required by state law
- That the tenant agrees to keep the property in good repair and not make any alterations without consent
- Tenant has inspected the property and has noted any unsafe, damaged, or unclean conditions
- Tenant agrees not to conduct any business or store any dangerous material on the property and agrees to notify landlord of any problems with the property
- Tenant agrees to use the property only as a single family residence and only with a noted number of tenants
- Tenant agrees to comply with all applicable laws and regulations
- Tenant agrees not to have any pets without permission of the landlord
- That landlord and tenant agree on who will pay utilities
- That the tenant agrees not to assign the lease or sublet the property without the landlord's consent
- That the landlord has the right to inspect the property on a reasonable basis,
- That the landlord has the right to re-enter and take possession upon breach of the lease (as long as it is in accordance with state law)
- Once the lease term has expired, any continued occupancy will be as a month-to month tenancy
- Landlord makes a required statement regarding radon gas

- Landlord discloses information regarding lead paint and tenant acknowledges receipt of this information and the following pamphlet
- That the landlord will provide tenant with the U.S. EPA lead pamphlet: "Protect Your Family from Lead in Your Home." *Note*: This document is provided on the Forms-on-CD and is necessary *only* if the rental dwelling was built prior to 1978
- Any other additional terms that the parties agree upon
- That any required notices must be sent to the landlord's and tenant's addresses as noted in the lease itself
- Finally, this lease notes that the landlord and tenant agree that the lease is the entire agreement and that it binds both landlord and tenant and any successors to the lease, that if there is any lawsuit to enforce the lease, whoever wins will pay the other parties legal fees and costs, and that the lease is governed by the laws of a particular state.

Note: You will also need to supply your tenant with a copy of the federal form: "Protect Your Family from Lead in Your Home" if the property was built prior to 1978. This form is included in Chapter 5 and on the Forms-on-CD. Residents of California will need to include the California Addendum to Lease form. Residents of Chicago will need to include the Chicago Addendum to Lease and other required Chicago forms. Residents of Florida will need to included the Florida Attachment to Lease Regarding Security Deposits. These forms are included in this chapter and on the Forms-on-CD. Residents of Florida, Maryland, and Michigan will need to add additional language to the lease form and must use the text formatted version of this lease on the Forms-on-CD in order to do so. Residents of all states should check the Appendix for any applicable provisions of their own state's laws.

If you wish to alter any of the terms of this lease or add additional terms, you will need to use the text formatted version of this lease on the Forms-on-CD.

To prepare this form, fill in the following information:

1. Date of lease
2. Name and address of landlord
3. Name and address of tenant
4. Complete address of leased property
5. Beginning and end date of lease
6. Amount of the rental payment
7. Period for which each rental payment will be due (usually, month)
8. Day of the period when rent will be due
9. Due date of first rental payment
10. Percentage of rent that will be applied to the purchase price of the property if option is exercised by tenant

⑪ Date option period expires

⑫ Anticipated purchase price of property

⑬ Anticipated rental payment deposit held in trust for option (use full term of lease amount)

⑭ Type and amount of any other deposit

⑮ Balance of purchase price due at closing

⑯ Total purchase price

⑰ Amount of mortgage commitment required

⑱ Number of monthly payments of mortgage commitment

⑲ Annual interest rate of mortgage commitment

⑳ Amount of late rent penalty (Check Appendix for any restrictions)

㉑ State in which property is located

㉒ Amount of returned check penalty

㉓ Amount of security deposit for damages

㉔ Number of days after lease termination when deposit must be returned to tenant

㉕ State in which property is located

㉖ If required, name, address, and possibly account number of where deposit is held (Check Appendix for your state)

㉗ Any items tenant has found that are not safe, clean or in good condition

㉘ Maximum number of tenants

㉙ State in which property is located

㉚ Utilities that landlord will supply

㉛ Utilities that tenant will provide

㉜ State in which property is located

㉝ State in which property is located

㉞ Landlord's initials on lead paint hazards and on records and/or reports of lead paint

㉟ Tenant's initials on lead paint acknowledgment

㊱ Any other additional terms

㊲ State where property is located

㊳ Signature of landlord

㊴ Printed name of landlord

㊵ Signature of tenant

㊶ Printed name of tenant

Lease with Purchase Option

This lease is made on ①_____ , 20 ①_____ , between
②_____ , landlord,
address: ②_____

and ③_____ , tenant,
address: ③_____

1. The Landlord agrees to rent to the Tenant and the Tenant agrees to rent from the Landlord the following residence: ④

2. The term of this lease will be from ⑤_____ , until ⑤_____ .

3. The rental payments will be $ ⑥_____ per ⑦_____ and will be payable by the Tenant to the Landlord on the ⑧_____ day of each month, beginning on ⑨_____ .

4. The Landlord agrees to give the Tenant an exclusive option to buy this property for the following price and terms:

   A. ⑩_____ percent of the amount that the Tenant pays the Landlord as rent under this Lease will be held as a deposit and credited against the purchase price of this property if this option is exercised by the Tenant. If the option is not exercised, the Seller will retain all of these payments as rent under this Lease.

   B. The option period will be from the beginning date of this Lease until ⑪_____ _____ , at which time it will expire unless exercised.

   C. During this period, the Tenant has the exclusive option and right to buy the leased property for the purchase price of $ ⑫_____ . The Tenant must notify the Landlord, in writing, of the decision to exercise this option. The purchase price will be paid as follows:

Rental payment deposit, to be held in trust by Landlord $ ⑬ _____
Other deposit: ⑭ _____ $ ⑭ _____
Cash or certified check for balance on closing $ ⑮ _____
(subject to any adjustments or prorations on closing)
Total Purchase Price $ ⑯ _____

D. Should the Tenant exercise this Option in writing, Landlord and Tenant agree to enter into a standard Agreement for the Sale of Real Estate. The Agreement will be conditional upon the Tenant being able to arrange suitable financing on the following terms at least thirty (30) days prior to the closing date specified in the Agreement for the Sale of Real Estate: a mortgage in the amount of ⑰ _____ , payable in ⑱ _____ monthly payments, with an annual interest rate of ⑲ _____ percent.

5. If the rental payment is late, the tenant agrees to pay an additional charge of $ ⑳ _____ per day as late rent penalty, except as limited by the laws of the State of ㉑ _____ .

6. If any check offered by the tenant is returned for insufficient funds, the tenant agrees to pay the landlord a returned check charge of $ ㉒ _____ .

7. The tenant has paid the landlord a security deposit of $ ㉓ _____ . This security deposit will be held as security for a). the repair of any damages to the residence by the tenant beyond normal wear and tear and/or b). cleaning the residence to the condition property was in upon moving in and/or c). non-payment of rent. This deposit will be returned to the tenant within ㉔ _____ days of the termination of this lease, minus any amounts needed to repair or clean the residence or for unpaid rent, but without interest, except as required by law in the State of ㉕ _____ .
Tenant agrees that if any damages to the property (caused by tenant or tenant's guests misuse or neglect of the property) are greater than this security deposit, then tenant shall pay for any additional damages. This deposit may NOT be applied by tenant to the tenant's last month's rent. If required by law, the security deposit will be held in the following account: ㉖ _____

_____ .

8. Tenant agrees to maintain the residence in a clean and sanitary manner and not to make any alterations to the residence without the landlord's written consent, except as required by law. At the termination of this lease, the tenant agrees to leave the residence in the same condition as when it was received, except for normal wear and tear.

9. Tenant has inspected the premises and found them to be in good, safe and clean condition, unless noted here: ㉗

10. Tenant also agrees not to conduct any type of business in the residence, nor store or use any dangerous or hazardous materials. Tenant agrees that the landlord will be notified immediately of any damages, defects, or dangerous conditions regarding the property.

11. Tenant agrees that the residence is to be used only as a single family residence, with a maximum of _____28_____ tenants.

12. Tenant also agrees to comply with all rules, laws, and ordinances affecting the residence, including all laws of the State of 29_____.

13. Tenant agrees that no pets or other animals are allowed in the residence without the written permission of the Landlord.

14. The landlord agrees to supply the following utilities to the tenant: 30

15. The tenant agrees to obtain and pay for the following utilities: 31

16. Tenant agrees not to sublet the residence or assign this lease without the landlord's written consent.

17. Tenant agrees to allow the landlord reasonable access to the residence for inspection and repair. Landlord agrees to enter the residence only after notifying the tenant in advance, except in an emergency, and according to the laws of the State of 32_____.

18. If the tenant fails to pay the rent on time or violates any other terms of this lease, the landlord will have the right to terminate this lease in accordance with state law. The landlord will also have the right to re-enter the residence and take possession of it and to take advantage of any other legal remedies available under the laws of the State of 33_____.

19. If the Tenant remains as tenant after the expiration of this lease without signing a new lease, a month-to-month tenancy will be created with the same terms and conditions as this lease, except that such new tenancy may be terminated by thirty (30) days written notice from either the Tenant or the Landlord.

20. As required by law, the landlord makes the following statement: "Radon gas is a naturally occurring radioactive gas that, when accumulated in sufficient quantities in a building, may present health risks to persons exposed to it. Levels of radon gas that exceed federal and

state guidelines have been found in buildings in this state. Additional information regarding radon gas and radon gas testing may be obtained from your county health department."

21. As required by law, the landlord makes the following **LEAD WARNING STATEMENT**:

"Every purchaser or lessee of any interest in residential real property on which a residential dwelling was built prior to 1978 is notified that such property may present exposure to lead from lead-based paint that may place young children at risk of developing lead poisoning. Lead poisoning in young children may produce permanent neurological damage, including learning disabilities, reduced intelligence quotient, behavioral problems, and impaired memory. Lead poisoning also poses a particular threat to pregnant women. The seller or lessor of any interest in residential real estate is required to provide the buyer with any information on lead-based paint hazards from risk assessments or inspection in the seller's or lessor's possession and notify the buyer or lessee of any known lead-based paint hazards. A risk assessment or inspection for possible lead-based paint hazards is recommended prior to purchase."

Landlord's Disclosure

Presence of lead-based paint and/or lead-based paint hazards: (Landlord to initial one).

___(34)___ Known lead-based paint and/or lead-based paint hazards are present in building (explain):

___(34)___ Landlord has no knowledge of lead-based paint and/or lead-based paint hazards in building.

Records and reports available to landlord: (Landlord to initial one).

___(34)___ Landlord has provided tenant with all available records and reports pertaining to lead-based paint and/or lead-based paint hazards are present in building (list documents):

___(34)___ Landlord has no records and reports pertaining to lead-based paint and/or lead-based paint hazards in building.

Tenant's Acknowledgment

(Tenant to initial all applicable).

___(35)___ Tenant has received copies of all information listed above.

___(35)___ Tenant has received the pamphlet "Protect Your Family from Lead in Your Home."

___(35)___ Tenant has received a ten (10)-day opportunity (or mutually agreed on period) to conduct a risk assessment or inspection for the presence of lead-based paint and/or lead-based paint hazards in building.

___(35)___ Tenant has waived the opportunity to conduct a risk assessment or inspection for the presence of lead-based paint and/or lead-based paint hazards in building.

The landlord and tenant have reviewed the information above and certify, by their signatures at the end of this lease, to the best of their knowledge, that the information they have provided is true and accurate.

22. The following are additional terms of this lease: (36)

23. The parties agree that this lease is the entire agreement between them.

24. Any required notices must be sent to the landlord's and tenant's addresses first noted to be valid.

25. This lease binds and benefits both the landlord and tenant and any successors.

26. In any legal proceeding to enforce any part of this lease, the prevailing party shall recover reasonable court costs and attorney's fees.

27. This lease is governed by the laws of the State of __(37)___ .

(38) _____
Signature of Landlord

(40) _____
Signature of Tenant

(39) _____
Printed Name of Landlord

(41) _____
Printed Name of Tenant

Month to Month Rental Agreement: This rental agreement provides for a month-to-month tenancy: one that continues each month indefinitely or until terminated by either party. For a fixed tenancy lease, please see the Residential Lease, explained above. Although the landlord and tenant can agree to any terms they desire, this particular lease provides for the following basic terms to be included:

- A month-to-month tenancy for the agreement
- A late payment fee is agreed to
- A returned check fee is agreed to
- A security deposit for damages, cleaning or unpaid rent, which will be returned to tenant after the termination of the lease, with any charges deducted, but without interest unless required by state law
- That the tenant agrees to keep the property in good repair and not make any alterations without consent
- Tenant has inspected the property and has noted any unsafe, damaged, or unclean conditions
- Tenant agrees not to conduct any business or store any dangerous material on the property and agrees to notify landlord of any problems with the property
- Tenant agrees to use the property only as a single family residence and only with a noted number of tenants
- Tenant agrees to comply with all applicable laws and regulations
- Tenant agrees not to have any pets without permission of the landlord
- That landlord and tenant agree on who will pay utilities
- That the tenant agrees not to assign the lease or sublet the property without the landlord's consent
- That the landlord has the right to inspect the property on a reasonable basis,
- That the landlord has the right to re-enter and take possession upon breach of the lease (as long as it is in accordance with state law)
- Once the lease term has expired, any continued occupancy will be as a month-to month tenancy
- Landlord makes a required statement regarding radon gas
- Landlord discloses information regarding lead paint and tenant acknowledges receipt of this information and the following pamphlet
- That the landlord will provide tenant with the U.S. EPA lead pamphlet: "Protect Your Family from Lead in Your Home." *Note*: This document is provided on the Forms-on-CD and is necessary *only* if the rental dwelling was built prior to 1978
- Any other additional terms that the parties agree upon
- That any required notices must be sent to the landlord's and tenant's addresses as noted in the lease itself
- Finally, this lease notes that the landlord and tenant agree that the lease is the entire agreement and that it binds both landlord and tenant and any successors

to the lease, that if there is any lawsuit to enforce the lease, whoever wins will pay the other parties legal fees and costs, and that the lease is governed by the laws of a particular state.

Note: You will also need to supply your tenant with a copy of the federal form: "Protect Your Family from Lead in Your Home" if the property was built prior to 1978. This form is included in Chapter 5 and on the Forms-on-CD. Residents of California will need to include the California Addendum to Lease form. Residents of Chicago will need to include the Chicago Addendum to Lease and other required Chicago forms. Residents of Florida will need to included the Florida Attachment to Lease Regarding Security Deposits. These forms are included in this chapter and on the Forms-on-CD. Residents of Florida, Maryland, and Michigan will need to add additional language to the lease form and must use the text formatted version of this lease on the Forms-on-CD in order to do so. Residents of all states should check the Appendix for any applicable provisions of their own state's laws.

If you wish to alter any of the terms of this lease or add additional terms, you will need to use the text formatted version of this lease on the Forms-on-CD. To prepare this form, fill in the following information:

To prepare this form, fill in the following information:

① Date of lease
② Name and address of landlord
③ Name and address of tenant
④ Complete address of leased property
⑤ Beginning date of lease
⑥ Number of days agreement can be terminated
⑦ Amount of the rental payment
⑧ Length of period (usually, month)
⑨ Day of the period when rent will be due
⑩ Due date of first rental payment
⑪ Amount of daily late charge (Note: some states restrict this amount–See Appendix)
⑫ State in which property is located
⑬ Amount of charge for returned check
⑭ Amount of security deposit for damages, cleaning or unpaid rent (Check Appendix)
⑮ Number of days to return deposit to tenant after end of lease (Check Appendix)
⑯ State in which property is located

㉗ If required: name, address, and possibly account # for holding deposit (Check Appendix)

⑱ Tenant's list of problems with property (based on pre-lease inspection)

⑲ Maximum number of tenants

⑳ State in which property is located

㉑ Utilities that landlord will supply

㉒ Utilities that tenant will provide

㉓ State in which property is located

㉔ State in which property is located

㉕ Landlord's initials on presence of lead paint disclosure

㉖ Landlord's initials on records and/or reports of lead paint

㉗ Tenant's initials on lead paint acknowledgment

㉘ Any other additional terms

㉙ Which state's laws will be used to interpret lease

㉚ Signature of landlord

㉛ Printed name of landlord

㉜ Signature of tenant

㉝ Printed name of tenant

Month to Month Rental Agreement

This Agreement is made on ① _____ , 20 ① ____ , between

② _____ , landlord,

address: ②

and ③ _____ , tenant,

address: ③

1. The Landlord agrees to rent to the Tenant and the Tenant agrees to rent from the Landlord on a month-to-month basis, the following residence: ④

2. This Agreement will begin on ⑤ _____ and will continue on a month-to-month basis until terminated. This agreement may only be terminated by ⑥ _____ days written notice from either party.

3. The rental payments will be $ ⑦ _____ per ⑧ _____ and will be payable by the tenant to the landlord on the ⑨ _____ day of each month, beginning on ⑩ _____ , 20 ⑩ ____ .

4. If the rental payment is late, the tenant agrees to pay an additional charge of $ ⑪ _____ per day as late rent penalty, except as limited by the laws of the State of ⑫ _____ .

5. If any check offered by the tenant is returned for insufficient funds, the tenant agrees to pay the landlord a returned check charge of $ ⑬ _____ .

6. The tenant has paid the landlord a security deposit of $ ⑭ _____ . This security deposit will be held as security for a). the repair of any damages to the residence by the tenant beyond normal wear and tear and/or b). cleaning the residence to the condition property was in upon moving in and/or c). non-payment of rent. This deposit will be returned to the tenant within ⑮ _____ days of the termination of this lease, minus any amounts needed to repair or clean the residence or for unpaid rent, but without interest, except as required by law in the State of ⑯ _____ .
    Tenant agrees that if any damages to the property (caused by tenant or tenant's guests misuse or neglect of the property) are greater than this security deposit, then tenant shall pay for any additional damages. This deposit may NOT be applied by tenant to the tenant's

last month's rent. If required by law, the security deposit will be held in the following account: ___⑰_____

_____.

7. Tenant agrees to maintain the residence in a clean and sanitary manner and not to make any alterations to the residence without the landlord's written consent, except as required by law. At the termination of this lease, the tenant agrees to leave the residence in the same condition as when it was received, except for normal wear and tear.

8. Tenant has inspected the premises and found them to be in good, safe and clean condition, unless noted here: ⑱

9. Tenant also agrees not to conduct any type of business in the residence, nor store or use any dangerous or hazardous materials. Tenant agrees that the landlord will be notified immediately of any damages, defects, or dangerous conditions regarding the property.

10. Tenant agrees that the residence is to be used only as a single family residence, with a maximum of _⑲_____ tenants.

11. Tenant also agrees to comply with all rules, laws, and ordinances affecting the residence, including all laws of the State of _⑳_____.

12. Tenant agrees that no pets or other animals are allowed in the residence without the written permission of the Landlord.

13. The landlord agrees to supply the following utilities to the tenant: ㉑

14. The tenant agrees to obtain and pay for the following utilities: ㉒

15. Tenant agrees not to sublet the residence or assign this lease without the landlord's written consent.

16. Tenant agrees to allow the landlord reasonable access to the residence for inspection and repair. Landlord agrees to enter the residence only after notifying the tenant in advance, except in an emergency, and according to the laws of the State of _㉓_____.

17. If the tenant fails to pay the rent on time or violates any other terms of this lease, the landlord will have the right to terminate this lease in accordance with state law. The landlord will also have the right to re-enter the residence and take possession of it and to take advantage of any other legal remedies available under the laws of the State of ㉔ _____.

18. If the Tenant remains as tenant after the expiration of this lease without signing a new lease, a month-to-month tenancy will be created with the same terms and conditions as this lease, except that such new tenancy may be terminated by thirty (30) days written notice from either the Tenant or the Landlord.

19. As required by law, the landlord makes the following statement: "Radon gas is a naturally occurring radioactive gas that, when accumulated in sufficient quantities in a building, may present health risks to persons exposed to it. Levels of radon gas that exceed federal and state guidelines have been found in buildings in this state. Additional information regarding radon gas and radon gas testing may be obtained from your county health department."

20. As required by law, the landlord makes the following **LEAD WARNING STATEMENT**:

"Every purchaser or lessee of any interest in residential real property on which a residential dwelling was built prior to 1978 is notified that such property may present exposure to lead from lead-based paint that may place young children at risk of developing lead poisoning. Lead poisoning in young children may produce permanent neurological damage, including learning disabilities, reduced intelligence quotient, behavioral problems, and impaired memory. Lead poisoning also poses a particular threat to pregnant women. The seller or lessor of any interest in residential real estate is required to provide the buyer with any information on lead-based paint hazards from risk assessments or inspection in the seller's or lessor's possession and notify the buyer or lessee of any known lead-based paint hazards. A risk assessment or inspection for possible lead-based paint hazards is recommended prior to purchase."

Landlord's Disclosure

Presence of lead-based paint and/or lead-based paint hazards: (Landlord to initial one).

㉕ _____ Known lead-based paint and/or lead-based paint hazards are present in building (explain):

㉕ _____ Landlord has no knowledge of lead-based paint and/or lead-based paint hazards in building.

Records and reports available to landlord: (Landlord to initial one).

___(26)___ Landlord has provided tenant with all available records and reports pertaining to lead-based paint and/or lead-based paint hazards are present in building (list documents):

___(26)___ Landlord has no records and reports pertaining to lead-based paint and/or lead-based paint hazards in building.

Tenant's Acknowledgment

(Tenant to initial all applicable).

___(27)___ Tenant has received copies of all information listed above.

___(27)___ Tenant has received the pamphlet "Protect Your Family from Lead in Your Home."

___(27)___ Tenant has received a ten (10)-day opportunity (or mutually agreed on period) to conduct a risk assessment or inspection for the presence of lead-based paint and/or lead-based paint hazards in building.

___(27)___ Tenant has waived the opportunity to conduct a risk assessment or inspection for the presence of lead-based paint and/or lead-based paint hazards in building.

The landlord and tenant have reviewed the information above and certify, by their signatures at the end of this lease, to the best of their knowledge, that the information they have provided is true and accurate.

21. The following are additional terms of this lease: (28)

22. The parties agree that this lease is the entire agreement between them.

23. Any required notices must be sent to the landlord's and tenant's addresses first noted to be valid.

24. This lease binds and benefits both the landlord and tenant and any successors.

25. In any legal proceeding to enforce any part of this lease, the prevailing party shall recover reasonable court costs and attorney's fees.

26. This lease is governed by the laws of the State of ㉙ _____ .

㉚ _____

Signature of Landlord

㉜ _____

Signature of Tenant

㉛ _____

Printed Name of Landlord

㉝ _____

Printed Name of Tenant

Addendum to Lease-California: The following form is required to be included as an attachment to all residential leases in the state of California. This form provides the required notice to tenants of the existence of a public access data base of the names and addresses of registered sexual offenders.

To complete this form, fill in the following information and attach it to the lease:

① Date of addendum (should generally be the same date as the lease)
② Name and address of landlord
③ Name and address of tenant
④ Date of lease
⑤ Complete address of leased property
⑥ Signature of landlord
⑦ Printed name of landlord
⑧ Signature of tenant
⑨ Printed name of tenant

Addendum to Lease-California

This Addendum to Lease is made on ①_____ , 20 ①____ ,
between ②_____ , landlord,
address: ②

and ③_____ , tenant,
address: ③

For valuable consideration, the parties agree as follows:

1. This Addendum is added to the following described lease, dated ④_____ , which is
   attached, and this Addendum is made a part of that lease: ⑤

2. The parties agree to add to this lease as follows:

Notice: The California Department of Justice, sheriff's departments, police departments serving
jurisdictions of 200,000 or more and many other local law enforcement authorities maintain for
public access a data base of the locations of persons required to register pursuant to paragraph
(1) of subdivision (a) of Section 290.4 of the Penal Code. The data base is updated on a quarterly
basis and a source of information about the presence of these individuals in any neighborhood. The
Department of Justice also maintains a Sex Offender Identification Line through which inquiries
about individuals may be made. This is a "900" telephone service. Callers must have specific
information about individuals they are checking. Information regarding neighborhoods is not
available through the "900" telephone service.

3. All other terms and conditions of the original lease remain in effect without further modification.
   This Addendum binds and benefits both parties and any successors. This document, including
   the attached lease, is the entire agreement between the parties.

The parties have signed this Addendum on the date specified at the beginning of this Addendum
of Lease.

⑥_____   ⑧_____
Signature of landlord   Signature of tenant

⑦_____   ⑨_____
Printed name of landlord   Printed name of tenant

Addendum to Lease-Chicago: The following form is required to be included as an attachment to all residential leases in the City of Chicago. This form provides the required notice to tenants that the landlord will supply the tenant with a copy of Chicago's Residential Landlord and Tenant Ordinance Summary (which follows this form). This form also provides for a heating cost disclosure and that the landlord will supply the tenant with a copy of the required Chicago Heating Cost Disclosure form (this disclosure also follows this form). All of these forms are supplied on the Forms-on-CD.

To complete this form, fill in the following information and attach it to the lease:

① Date of addendum (should generally be the same date as the lease)
② Name and address of landlord
③ Name and address of tenant
④ Date of lease
⑤ Complete address of leased property
⑥ The projected average monthly cost of heating utility bills for the property
⑦ Signature of landlord
⑧ Printed name of landlord
⑨ Signature of tenant
⑩ Printed name of tenant

Addendum to Lease-Chicago

This Addendum to Lease is made on ① _____ , 20 _____ ,
between ② _____ , landlord,
address:

and ③ _____ , tenant,
address:

For valuable consideration, the parties agree as follows:

1. This Addendum is added to the following described lease, dated ④ _____ , which is attached, and this Addendum is made a part of that lease: ⑤

2. The parties agree to add to this lease as follows:

Landlord shall supply tenant with a copy of Chicago's Residential Landlord and Tenant Ordinance Summary.

Additionally, if Tenant is responsible for heating of the rental unit, Landlord agrees to supply the Tenant with the average monthly cost of heating the rental unit during normal weather on the attached Heating Cost Disclosure Form. In addition, the following disclosure applies:

Heating Cost Disclosure (for Tenant-Heated Apartments)
For all properties to which the Heating Cost Disclosure Ordinance (Chicago, IL Municipal Code, Chapter 193.21) is applicable.
    a. The cost of heating the apartment shall be the responsibility of Tenant.
    b. Tenant acknowledges that Tenant was provided with heating cost information prior to any written or verbal agreement to enter into this lease and prior to any exchange of money. The projected average monthly cost of heat utility service (based on energy consumption during the most recent Annual Period by continuous occupancy by one or more occupants, current or estimated rates and normal weather) for the Apartment is $ ⑥ _____ .
    c. A copy of the Heating Cost Disclosure Form as required by the City of Chicago Department of Consumer Services is attached to this lease.
    d. By signing this lease, Tenant acknowledges that tenant has received the Heating Cost Disclosure Form.

3. All other terms and conditions of the original lease remain in effect without further modification. This Addendum binds and benefits both parties and any successors. This document, including the attached lease, is the entire agreement between the parties.

The parties have signed this Addendum on the date specified at the beginning of this Ad‹ of Lease.

⑦ _____
Signature of landlord

⑧ _____
Printed name of landlord

⑨ _____
Signature of tenant

⑩ _____
Printed name of tenant

CITY OF CHICAGO	CITY OF CHICAGO
RICHARD M. DALEY, MAYOR	DEPARTMENT OF CONSUMER SERVICES
	APPLICATION FOR ENERGY DISCLOSURE
CAROLINE ORZAC SHOENBERGER	THE PEOPLES GAS & COKE COMPANY
COMMISSIONER	COMMONWEALTH EDISON COMPANY

Separate applications are required for Gas and Electric Heat. Please check one box. Mail or fax completed form to the appropriate utility company as indicated below.

[ ] Gas Heat   [ ] Electric Heat

For all addresses   **For addresses mail request to:**
                                      ComEd

The Peoples Gas Light & Coke Company | Attn: Central Handling Group | You may also submit your request by
Attn: Energy Disclosure Section | 2100 Swift Drive | visiting their web site: www.ucm.com
130 East Randolph Drive, 16ᵗʰ Floor | Oak Brook, IL 60523 | Select ComEd and send your request
Chicago, IL 60601 | Fax# (630) 684-2692 | via e-mail.
Voice (312) 240-4040 | Phone# 1-800-334-7661 |
Fax (312)240-3991 | |

****************PLEASE PRINT ***************

Owner or Realtor (Please Circle One _and_ List Complete Name)_____

Owner / Realtor Mailing Address_____Chicago, IL (Zip Code)_____

Owner / Realtor Telephone Number _____Agent's Name (if applicable)_____

Owner / Realtor Fax Number _____

Name Of Occupant (if different from the owner)_____

ADDRESS AND APARTMENT NUMBER OF DWELLING UNIT
Note: If dwelling has multiple addresses or is a corner building, list each address separately and the first and last apartment number at the bottom:

Example: 111 1 st ST.   Apt. 101-328
     113 1 st ST.   Apt. 329-528
Address (You must include direction)   **Apartment Number (S)**

_____   _____

_____   _____

_____   _____

_____   _____

_____   _____

_____   _____

Knowing that there are legal penalties for making a false claim of ownership or agency, I hereby certify that I am the owner / agent for the property in question, and I hereby request disclosure of the projected annual and projected average monthly cost of electricity or gas which provides the only source of heat for the above-described dwelling unit(s).

Date of request:_____ Signature:_____

For additional forms, you may contact the City of Chicago, Department of Consumer Services, at (312) 744-9400.

DO NOT MAIL TO THE DEPARTMENT OF CONSUMER SERVICES

CITY OF CHICAGO
RESIDENTIAL LANDLORD AND
TENANT ORDINANCE SUMMARY

City of Chicago
Richard M. Daley
Mayor

Chicago Department of Housing
John G. Markowski
Commissioner

At initial offering, this Summary of the ordinance must be attached to every written rental agreement and also upon initial offering for renewal. The Summary must also be given to a tenant at initial offering of an oral agreement, whether the agreement is new or a renewal. Unless otherwise noted, all provisions are effective as of November 6, 1986. {Mun. Code ch. 5-12-170}

> IMPORTANT: IF YOU SEEK TO EXERCISE RIGHTS UNDER THE ORDINANCE, OBTAIN A COPY OF THE ENTIRE ORDINANCE TO DETERMINE APPROPRIATE REMEDIES AND PROCEDURES. CONSULTING AN ATTORNEY WOULD ALSO BE ADVISABLE. FOR A COPY OF THE ORDINANCE, VISIT THE CITY CLERK'S OFFICE ROOM 107, CITY HALL, 121 N. LASALLE, CHICAGO ILLINOIS.

IMPORTANT NOTICE

A message about porch safety: The porch or deck of this building should be designed for a live load of up to 100 lbs. per square foot, and is safe only for its intended use. Protect your safety. Do not overload the porch or deck. If you have questions about porch or deck safety, call the City of Chicago non-emergency number, 3-1-1.

WHAT RENTAL UNITS ARE COVERED BY THE ORDINANCE? {MUN. CODE CH 5-12-010 & 5-12-020}

- Rental units with written or oral leases (including all subsidized units such as CHA, IHDA, Section 8 Housing Choice Vouchers, etc.)
 EXCEPT
- Units in owner occupied buildings with six or fewer units.
- Units in hotels, motels, rooming houses, unless rent is paid on a monthly basis and unit is occupied for more than 32 days.
- School dormitory rooms, shelters, employee's quarters, non-residential rental properties.
- Owner occupied co-ops and condominiums.

WHAT ARE THE TENANT'S GENERAL DUTIES UNDER THE ORDINANCE? {MUN. CODE CH. 5-12-040}

The tenant, the tenant's family and invited guests must comply with all obligations imposed specifically upon tenants by the Municipal Code, including:
- Buying and installing working batteries in smoke and carbon monoxide detectors within tenant's apartment.
- Keeping the unit safe and clean.
- Using all equipment and facilities in a reasonable manner.
- Not damaging the unit.
- Not disturbing other residents.

LANDLORD'S RIGHT OF ACCESS {MUN. CODE CH. 5-12-050}

- A tenant shall permit reasonable access to a landlord upon receiving two days notice by mail, telephone, written notice or other means designed in good faith to provide notice.
- A general notice to all affected tenants may be given in the event repair work on common areas or other units may require such access.
- In the event of emergency or where repairs elsewhere unexpectedly require access, the landlord must provide notice within two days after entry.

SECURITY DEPOSITS AND PREPAID RENT {MUN. CODE CH. 5-12-080 AND 5-12-081}

- A landlord must give a tenant a receipt for a security deposit including the owner's name, the date it was received and a description of the dwelling unit. The receipt must be signed by the person accepting the security deposit.
- A landlord must pay interest each year on security deposits and prepaid rent (eff. 1-1-92) held more than six months.
- The rate of interest a landlord must pay is set each year by the City Comptroller. (eff. 7-1-97)
- Before expenses for damages can be deducted from the security deposit, the landlord must provide the tenant with an itemized statement of the damages within 30 days of the date the tenant vacates the dwelling unit.
- A landlord must return all security deposit and required interest, if any, minus unpaid rent and expenses for damages, within 45 days from the date the tenant vacates the unit.

WHAT ARE THE LANDLORD'S GENERAL DUTIES UNDER THE ORDINANCE?

- To give tenant written notice of the owner's or manager's name, address and telephone number. {Mun. Code ch. 5-12-090}
- To give new or renewing tenants notice of:
  1) Code citations issued by the City in the previous 12 months;
  2) Pending Housing Court or administrative hearing actions;
  3) Water, electrical or gas service shut-offs to the building during entire occupancy. {Mun. Code ch. 5-12-100}
- To maintain the property in compliance with all applicable provisions of the Municipal Code. {Mun. Code ch. 5-12-070}
- To not require a tenant to renew an agreement more than 90 days before the existing agreement terminates. (eff. 1-1-92) {Mun. Code ch. 5-12-130 (j)}
- To provide a tenant with at least 30 days written notice if the rental agreement will not be renewed. If the landlord fails to give the required written notice, the tenant may remain in the dwelling unit for 60 days under the same terms and conditions as the last month of the existing agreement. (eff. 1-1-92) {Mun. Code ch. 5-12-130 (j)}
- To not enforce prohibited lease provisions. {Mun Code ch. 5-12-140}

TENANT REMEDIES {MUN. CODE CH. 5-12-110}

Minor Defects

- If the landlord fails to maintain the property in compliance with the Code and the tenant or the tenant's family or guests are not responsible for the failure, the tenant may:
  1) Request in writing that the landlord make repairs within 14 days, and if the landlord fails to do so the tenant may withhold an amount of rent that reasonably reflects the reduced value of the unit. Rent withholding begins from the fifteenth day until repairs are made; OR
  2) Request in writing that the landlord make repairs within 14 days and if the landlord fails to do so the tenant may have the repairs made and deduct up to $500 or 1/2 of the month's rent, whichever is more, but not to exceed one month's rent. Repairs must be done in compliance with the Code. Receipt for the repairs must be given to the landlord and no more than the cost of the repairs can be deducted from the rent; and also
  3) File suit against the landlord for damages and injunctive relief.

Major Defects

- If the landlord fails to maintain the property in compliance with the Code, and the failure renders the premises not reasonably fit and habitable, the tenant may request in writing that the landlord make repairs within 14 days. If after 14 days repairs are not made, the tenant may immediately terminate the lease. Tenant must deliver possession and move out in 30 days or tenant's notice is considered withdrawn. (eff. 1-1-92)

FAILURE TO PROVIDE ESSENTIAL SERVICES (HEAT, RUNNING OR HOT WATER, ELECTRICITY, GAS OR PLUMBING) {MUN. CODE CH. 5-12-110(F)}

- If, contrary to the lease, an essential service is not provided, or if the landlord fails to maintain the building in material compliance with the Code to such an extent that such failure constitutes an immediate danger to the health and safety of the tenant, and the tenant or tenant's family or guests are not responsible for such failure, after giving written notice, the tenant may do ONE of the following:
  1) Procure substitute service, and upon presenting paid receipts to the landlord, deduct the cost from the rent; OR
  2) File suit against the landlord and recover damages based on the reduced value of the dwelling unit; OR
  3) Procure substitute housing and be excused from paying rent for that period. The tenant may also recover from the landlord the cost of substitute housing up to an amount equal to the monthly rent for each month or portion thereof; OR
  4) Request that the landlord correct the failure within 24 hours and if the landlord fails to do so, withhold the monthly rent an amount that reasonable reflects the reduced value of its premises. Rent withholding cannot start until after the 24 hours expires and applies only to days past the 24-hour waiting period; OR (eff. 1-1-92)
  5) Request that the landlord correct the failure within 72 hours and if the landlord fails to do so, terminate the rental agreement. If the rental agreement is terminated, the tenant must deliver possession and move out within 30 days or the notice of termination is considered withdrawn. (eff. 1-1-92)

Note: Remedies 4) and 5) may not be used if the failure is due to the utility provider's failure to provide service. For the purposes of this section only, the notice a tenant provides must be in writing, delivered to the address the landlord has given the tenant as an address to which notices should be sent. If the landlord does not inform the tenant of an address, the tenant may deliver written notice to the last known address of the landlord or by any other reasonable means designed in good faith to provide written notice to the landlord. (eff.1-1-92)

FIRE OR CASUALTY DAMAGE {MUN. CH 5-12-110 (G)}

- If a fire damages the unit to an extent that it is in material noncompliance with the Code and the tenant, tenant's family or guests are not responsible for the fire or accident, the tenant may:

1) Move out immediately, but if this is done, the tenant must provide written notice to the landlord of the intention to terminate within 14 days after moving out.

2) The tenant may stay in the unit, if it is legal, but if the tenant stays and cannot use a portion of the unit because of damage, the rent may be reduced to reflect the reduced value of the unit.

3) If the tenant stays, and the landlord fails to diligently carry out the work, the tenant may notify the landlord, in writing, within 14 days after the tenant becomes aware that the work is not being diligently carried out, of the tenant's intention to terminate the rental agreement and move out.

SUBLEASES {MUN. CODE CH. 5-12-120}

- The landlord must accept a reasonable subtenant offered by the tenant without charging additional fees.
- If a tenant moves prior to the end of the rental agreement, the landlord must make a good faith effort to find a new tenant at a fair rent.
- If the landlord is unsuccessful in re-renting the unit, the tenant remains liable for the rent under the rental agreement, as well as the landlord's cost of advertising.

WHAT HAPPENS IF A TENANT PAYS RENT LATE? {MUN. CODE CH. 5-12-140 (h)}

- If the tenant fails to pay rent on time, the landlord may charge a late fee of $10.00 per month on rents under $500 plus 5 percent per month on that part of the rent that exceeds $500.00 (i.e., for a $450.00 monthly rent the late fee is $10.00, for a $700 monthly rent the late fee is $10 plus 5% of $200.00 or $20.00 total) (eff. 1-1-92)

WHAT HAPPENS IF A TENANT PAYS RENT DUE AFTER THE EXPIRATION OF THE TIME PERIOD SET FORTH IN A TERMINATION NOTICE? {MUN. CODE CH. 5-12-140 (h)}

- If the landlord accepts the rent due knowing that there is a default in payment, the tenant may stay.

LANDLORD REMEDIES {MUN. CODE CH. 5-12-130}

- If the tenant fails to pay rent, the landlord, after giving five days written notice to the tenant, may terminate the rental agreement.
- If the tenant fails to comply with the Code or the rental agreement, the landlord, after giving 10 days written notice to the tenant, may terminate the rental agreement if tenant fails to correct the violation.
- If the tenant fails to comply with the Code or the rental agreement, the landlord may request in writing that the tenant comply as promptly as conditions permit in the case of emergency, or within 14 days. If the breach is not corrected in the time period specified, the landlord may enter the dwelling unit and have the necessary work done. In this case, the tenant shall be responsible for all costs of repairs.

LOCKOUTS {MUN. CODE CH. 5-12-160}

This section applies to every residential rental unit in Chicago. There are no exceptions.
- It is illegal for a landlord to lock out a tenant, or change locks, or remove doors of a rental unit, or cut off heat, utility or water service, or to do anything which interferes with the tenant's use of the apartment.
- All lockouts are illegal and the Police Department is responsible for enforcement against such illegal activity. (eff. 1 1 92) (Police Special Order 93-12)
- The landlord shall be fined $200 to $500 for each day the lockout occurs or continues.
- The tenant may sue the landlord to recover possession of the unit and twice the actual damages sustained or two months' rent, whichever is greater.

PROHIBITION ON RETALIATORY CONDUCT BY LANDLORD {MUN. CODE CH. 5-12-150}

- A tenant has the right to complain or testify in good faith about their tenancy to governmental agencies or officials, police, media, community groups, tenant unions or the landlord. A landlord is prohibited from retaliating by terminating or threatening to terminate a tenancy, increasing rent, decreasing services, bringing or threatening to bring an eviction action, or refusing to renew a lease agreement.

ATTORNEY'S FEES {MUN. CODE CH. 5-12-180}

- Except in eviction actions, the prevailing plaintiff in any action arising from the application of this Ordinance shall be entitled to recover all court costs and reasonable attorney's fees. (eff. 1-1-92)

WHERE CAN I GET A COPY OF THE ORDINANCE?

- For a copy of the Ordinance, visit the Office of the City Clerk, Room 107, City Hall, 121 North LaSalle Street, Chicago, Illinois or view it at the Municipal Reference Library, Harold Washington Library, 5th Floor, 400 S. State Street, Chicago, Illinois.

Approved by the City of Chicago, January 2000   173158-bro-12-6

Florida Attachment to Lease Regarding Security Deposits: The following form is required to be included as an attachment to all residential leases in the State of Florida. This form provides the required notice to tenants regarding Florida law about the return of security deposits. This form is supplied on the Forms-on-CD. A copy of this form should be attached to the lease and language should be added in the "additional terms" section of the lease that "A copy of Florida Statutes regarding return of security deposits is attached to this lease."

To complete this form, fill in the following information and attach it to the lease:

① Amount of security deposit not returned
② Reason for deduction
③ Landlord address

Florida Attachment to Lease Regarding Security Deposits
Florida Statutes, Section 83.49(3)

(3)(a) Upon the vacating of the premises for termination of the lease, if the landlord does not intend to impose a claim on the security deposit, the landlord shall have 15 days to return the security deposit together with interest if otherwise required, or the landlord shall have 30 days to give the tenant written notice by certified mail to the tenant's last known mailing address of his or her intention to impose a claim on the deposit and the reason for imposing the claim. The notice shall contain a statement in substantially the following form:

This is a notice of my intention to impose a claim for damages in the amount of ① _____
upon your security deposit, due to ② _____ (reason for deduction). It is sent to you as required by s. 83.49(3), Florida Statutes. You are hereby notified that you must object in writing to this deduction from your security deposit within 15 days from the time you receive this notice or I will be authorized to deduct my claim from your security deposit. Your objection must be sent to ③ _____
_____ (landlord's address).

If the landlord fails to give the required notice within the 30-day period, he or she forfeits the right to impose a claim upon the security deposit.

(b) Unless the tenant objects to the imposition of the landlord's claim or the amount thereof within 15 days after receipt of the landlord's notice of intention to impose a claim, the landlord may then deduct the amount of his or her claim and shall remit the balance of the deposit to the tenant within 30 days after the date of the notice of intention to impose a claim for damages.

(c) If either party institutes an action in a court of competent jurisdiction to adjudicate the party's right to the security deposit, the prevailing party is entitled to receive his or her court costs plus a reasonable fee for his or her attorney. The court shall advance the cause on the calendar.

(d) Compliance with this section by an individual or business entity authorized to conduct business in this state, including Florida-licensed real estate brokers and sales associates, shall constitute compliance with all other relevant Florida Statutes pertaining to security deposits held pursuant to a rental agreement or other landlord-tenant relationship. Enforcement personnel shall look solely to this section to determine compliance. This section prevails over any conflicting provisions in chapter 475 and in other sections of the Florida Statutes, and shall operate to permit licensed real estate brokers to disburse security deposits and deposit money without having to comply with the notice and settlement procedures contained in Section 475.25(1)(d).

CHAPTER 3
Alterations to Real Estate Lease Forms

This chapter contains various forms that may be used to make alterations to the basic leases that were provided in the previous chapter. Changes to a lease may be required for a wide variety of reasons. The landlord and/or tenant may wish to amend a lease by adding or deleting a particular provision. An Amendment of Lease is provided for this. They may wish to extend a lease without the necessity of making an entirely new lease. An Extension of Lease is used for this purpose. If both the landlord and tenant agree, they may use the Mutual Termination of Lease to voluntarily end a lease. If for any reason, either party wishes to assign their rights under the lease to another party, an Assignment of Lease form may be used for this purpose. The leases in this book require that the consent of the landlord is required for a tenant to assign his or her rights under a lease to another person. A Consent to Assignment of Lease form is provided for this purpose. Finally, a tenant may wish to sublet the rented property to another person. A Sublease form is provided for this purpose. Again, the leases in this book require that the consent of the landlord is required for a tenant to sublet to another person. A Consent to Sublease form is provided for this purpose.

Prior to each form, a more detailed explanation of the purposes and uses of these forms is provided. In addition, a list of what information is necessary to complete each form is also provided.

Amendment of Lease: Use this form to modify any terms of a lease. A copy of the original lease should be attached to this form. The amendment can be used to change any portion of the lease. Simply note what changes are being made in the appropriate place on this form. If a portion of the lease is being deleted, make note of the deletion. If certain language is being substituted, state the substitution clearly. If additional language is being added, make this clear. For example, you may wish to use language as follows:

"Paragraph _____ is deleted from this lease."

"Paragraph _____ is deleted from this lease and the following paragraph is substituted in its place:

"The following new paragraph is added to this lease:"

In order to prepare this Amendment, please fill in the following information:

① Date of amendment
② Name of landlord and address
③ Name of tenant and address
④ Description of original lease (including date of lease and description of property involved)
⑤ Terms of amendment
⑥ Signature of landlord
⑦ Printed name of landlord
⑧ Signature of tenant
⑨ Printed name of tenant

Amendment of Lease

This amendment of lease is made on ①_____ , 20 ①_____ , between
②_____ , landlord,
address: ②

and ③_____ , tenant,
address: ③

For valuable consideration, the parties agree as follows:

1. The following described lease is attached to this amendment and is made a part of this amendment: ④

2. The parties agree to amend this lease as follows: ⑤

3. All other terms and conditions of the original lease remain in effect without modification. This amendment binds and benefits both parties and any successors. This document, including the attached lease, is the entire agreement between the parties.

The parties have signed this amendment on the date specified at the beginning of this amendment.

⑥_____   ⑧_____
Signature of Landlord   Signature of Tenant

⑦_____   ⑨_____
Printed Name of Landlord   Printed Name of Tenant

Extension of Lease: This document should be used to extend the effective time period during which a lease is in force. The use of this form allows the time limit to be extended without having to entirely re-draft the lease. Under this document, all of the other terms of the lease will remain the same, with only the expiration date changing. A copy of the original lease should be attached to this form.

To complete this form, fill in the following information:

① Date of extension
② Name of landlord and address
③ Name of tenant and address
④ Date on which original lease will end
⑤ Description of original lease (including date of lease and description of property involved)
⑥ Date on which extension of lease will end
⑦ Signature of landlord
⑧ Printed name of landlord
⑨ Signature of tenant
⑩ Printed name of tenant

Extension of Lease

This extension of lease is made on ___①_____ , 20 ①___ , between
___②_____ , landlord,
address: ②

and ___③_____ , tenant,
address: ③

For valuable consideration, the parties agree as follows:

1. The following described lease will end on ___④_____ , 20 ④___ : ⑤

    This lease is attached to this extension and is a part of this extension.

2. The parties agree to extend this lease for an additional period, which will begin
    immediately on the expiration of the original time period and will end on
    ___⑥_____ , 20 ⑥___ .

3. The extension of this lease will be on the same terms and conditions as the original lease.
    This extension binds and benefits both parties and any successors. This document, includ-
    ing the attached lease, is the entire agreement between the parties.

The parties have signed this extension on the date specified at the beginning of this extension.

⑦_____   ⑨_____
Signature of Landlord   Signature of Tenant

⑧_____   ⑩_____
Printed Name of Landlord   Printed Name of Tenant

Mutual Termination of Lease: This form should be used when both the landlord and tenant desire to terminate a lease. This document releases both parties from any claims that the other may have against them for any actions under the lease. It also states that the landlord agrees that the rent has been paid in full and that the property has been delivered in good condition.

To complete this form, fill in the following information:

1. Date of termination
2. Name of landlord and address
3. Name of tenant and address
4. Description of original lease (including date of lease and description of property involved)
5. Signature of landlord
6. Printed name of landlord
7. Signature of tenant
8. Printed name of tenant

Mutual Termination of Lease

This termination of lease is made on ①_____ , 20 ①____ , between
_②_____ , landlord,
address: ②_____

and ③_____ , tenant,
address: ③_____

For valuable consideration, the parties agree as follows:

1. The parties are currently bound under the terms of the following described lease: ④

2. They agree to mutually terminate and cancel this lease effective on this date. This termination agreement will act as a mutual release of all obligations under this lease for both parties, as if the lease has not been entered into in the first place. Landlord agrees that all rent due has been paid and that the possession of the property has been returned in satisfactory condition.

3. This termination binds and benefits both parties and any successors. This document, including the attached lease being terminated, is the entire agreement between the parties.

The parties have signed this termination on the date specified at the beginning of this termination.

⑤_____   ⑦_____
Signature of Landlord   Signature of Tenant

⑥_____   ⑧_____
Printed Name of Landlord   Printed Name of Tenant

Assignment of Lease: This form is for use if one party to a lease is assigning its full interest in the lease to another party. This effectively substitutes one party for another under a lease. This particular assignment form has both of the parties agreeing to indemnify and hold each other harmless for any failures to perform under the lease while they were the party liable under it. This Assignment of Lease may be used by a seller of real estate to assign their interest in any lease that covers the property for sale to the new buyer. This *indemnify and hold harmless* clause simply means that if a claim arises for failure to perform, each party agrees to be responsible for the period of their own performance obligations. A description of the lease which is assigned should include the parties to the lease, a description of the property, and the date of the lease. Other information that is necessary to complete the assignment is the name and address of the *assignor* (the party who is assigning the lease), the name and address of the *assignee* (the party to whom the lease is being assigned), and the date of the assignment. A copy of the original lease should be attached to this form.

In order to prepare this Assignment, please fill in the following information:

① Date of assignment
② Name of assignor
③ Address of assignor
④ Name of assignee
⑤ Address of assignee
⑥ Description of original lease (including date of lease and description of property involved)
⑦ Signature of assignor
⑧ Printed name of assignor
⑨ Signature of assignee
⑩ Printed name of assignee

Assignment of Lease

This assignment is made on ① _____ , 20 _____ , between
② _____ , assignor,
address: ③ _____

and ④ _____ , assignee,
address: ⑤ _____

For valuable consideration, the parties agree to the following terms and conditions:

1. The assignor assigns all interest, burdens, and benefits in the following described lease to the assignee: ⑥

    This lease is attached to this assignment and is a part of this assignment.

2. The assignor warrants that this lease is in effect, has not been modified, and is fully assignable. If the consent of the landlord is necessary for this assignment to be effective, such consent is attached to this assignment and is a part of this assignment. Assignor agrees to indemnify and hold the assignee harmless from any claim which may result from the assignor's failure to perform under this lease prior to the date of this assignment.

3. The assignee agrees to perform all of the obligations of the assignor and receive all of the benefits of the assignor under this lease. Assignee agrees to indemnify and hold the assignor harmless from anyclaim which may result from the assignee's failure to perform under this lease after the date of this assignment.

4. This assignment binds and benefits both parties and any successors. This document, including any attachments, is the entire agreement between the parties.

⑦ _____   ⑨ _____
Signature of Assignor   Signature of Assignee

⑧ _____   ⑩ _____
Printed Name of Assignor   Printed Name of Assignee

Consent to Assignment of Lease: This form is used if the original lease states that the consent of the landlord is necessary for the assignment of the lease to be valid. A landlord may wish to supply a copy of this form to a tenant if a tenant requests the landlord's consent for an assignment of the lease to another party. A copy of the original lease should be attached to this form.

To complete this form, the following information is needed:

① Date of consent to assignment
② Name of tenant requesting consent
③ Address of tenant requesting consent
④ Name of tenant requesting consent
⑤ Description of lease, including date of lease and location of leased premises
⑥ Signature of landlord
⑦ Printed name of landlord

Consent to Assignment of Lease

Date: ① _____ , 20 _____

To: ②
    ③

RE: Assignment of Lease

Dear ④ _____ :

I am the landlord under the following described lease: ⑤

This lease is the subject of the attached assignment of lease.

I consent to the assignment of this lease as described in the attached assignment, which provides that the assignee is fully substituted for the assignor.

⑥ _____
Signature of Landlord

⑦ _____
Printed Name of Landlord

Sublease: This form is used if the tenant subleases the property covered by an original lease. This particular sublease form has both of the parties agreeing to indemnify and hold each other harmless for any failures to perform under the lease while they were the party liable under it. This *indemnify and hold harmless* clause simply means that if a claim arises for failure to perform, each party agrees to be responsible for the period of their own performance obligations. A description of the lease which is subleased should include the parties to the lease, a description of the property, and the date of the lease. Note that the *subtenant* is the party to whom the property is being subleased. A copy of the original lease should be attached to this form. A copy of a Consent to Sublease of Lease should also be attached, if necessary.

To complete this form, enter the following information:

① Date of sublease
② Name of tenant
③ Address of tenant
④ Name of subtenant
⑤ Address of subtenant
⑥ Description of property covered by lease
⑦ Description of original lease (including date of lease and name and address of landlord)
⑧ Beginning date of sublease
⑨ Ending date of sublease
⑩ Amount of subrental payments
⑪ Period for each subrental payment (generally, per month)
⑫ Day of month each subrental payment is due
⑬ Beginning date for first subrental payment
⑭ Any additional terms of sublease
⑮ State law which will govern the sublease
⑯ Signature of tenant
⑰ Printed name of tenant
⑱ Signature of subtenant
⑲ Printed name of subtenant

Sublease

This sublease is made on ① _____ , 20 _____ , between
② _____ , tenant,
address: ③ _____

and ④ _____ , subtenant,
address: ⑤ _____

For valuable consideration, the parties agree to the following terms and conditions:

1. The tenant subleases to the subtenant the following described property: ⑥

2. This property is currently leased to the tenant under the terms of the following described lease: ⑦

    This lease is attached to this sublease and is a part of this sublease.

3. This sublease will be for the period from ⑧ _____ , 20 ⑧ _____ , to
    ⑨ _____ , 20 ⑨ _____ .

4. The subrental payments will be $ ⑩ _____ per ⑪ _____ and will
    be payable by the subtenant to the landlord on the ⑫ _____ day of each month,
    beginning on ⑬ _____ , 20 ⑬ _____ .

5. The tenant warrants that the underlying lease is in effect, has not been modified, and that the property may be sublet. If the consent of the landlord is necessary for his sublease to be effective, such consent is attached to this sublease and is a part of this sublease. Tenant agrees to indemnify and hold the subtenant harmless from any claim which may result from the tenant's failure to perform under this lease prior to the date of this sublease.

6. The subtenant agrees to perform all of the obligations of the tenant under the original lease and receive all of the benefits of the tenant under this lease. Subtenant agrees to indemnify and hold the tenant harmless from any claim which may result from the subtenant's failure to perform under this lease after the date of this sublease.

7. The tenant agrees to remain primarily liable to the landlord for the obligations under the lease.

8. The parties agree to the following additional terms: ⑭

9. This sublease binds and benefits both parties and any successors. This document, including any attachments, is the entire agreement between the parties. This sublease is subject to the laws of the State of ⑮_____.

⑯ _____
Signature of Tenant

⑱ _____
Signature of Subtenant

⑰ _____
Printed Name of Tenant

⑲ _____
Printed Name of Subtenant

Consent to Sublease of Lease: This form is used if the original lease states that the consent of the landlord is necessary for a sublease to be valid. A landlord may wish to supply a copy of this form to a tenant if a tenant requests the landlord's consent for a sublease of the lease to another party. A copy of the original lease should be attached to this form and a copy should be attached to any sublease of a property.

To complete this form, the following information is needed:

① Date of consent to sublease
② Name of tenant requesting consent
③ Address of tenant requesting consent
④ Name of tenant requesting consent
⑤ Description of lease, including date of lease and location of leased premises
⑥ Signature of landlord
⑦ Printed name of landlord

Consent to Sublease of Lease

Date: ① _____ , 20 ① ____

To ②
③

RE: Sublease of Lease

Dear ④ _____ :

I am the landlord under the following described lease: ⑤

This lease is the subject of the attached sublease.

I consent to the sublease of this lease as described in the attached sublease, which provides that the subtenant is substituted for the tenant for the period indicated in the sublease. This consent does not release the tenant from any obligations under the lease and the tenant remains fully bound under the lease.

⑥
_____
Signature of Landlord

⑦
_____
Printed Name of Landlord

CHAPTER 4
Notices Relating to Real Estate Leases

This chapter contains a variety of forms that may be used for providing notice to tenants for various reasons: that rent is overdue, that the landlord needs to enter the property to inspect or repair the property, that some type of service to the property has occurred (such as checking the furnace or plumbing), and a number of other notices. The use of these notices provides an effective method by which a landlord may both provide written notices to the tenant of certain actions or activities and also provide a clear record of the landlord's own actions relating to the tenant.

Note Regarding Evictions: The eviction of a tenant from a property is a matter of state law and, often, municipal regulations. The laws relating to evictions are often complex and filled with critical deadlines and technicalities. Because of the complex and local nature of eviction laws, it is not feasible to provide the forms and details for eviction law for all 50 states and the many municipalities that have additional regulations. Although several of the notices in this chapter may be used in eviction situations, they are not intended to be used in such a manner unless the landlord has a thorough knowledge of eviction law or has had competent legal advice from an attorney skilled in landlord/tenant law.

In general, a landlord has the right to obtain possession of a rented property if the tenant has violated the terms of the lease (for example, by failure to pay rent, by continuing to occupy the property after the lease has expired, or some other express violation of clear terms of the lease). However, in order to obtain possession of the property, the tenant must either abandon the property or voluntarily surrender possession of the property to the landlord. If the tenant neither abandons nor surrenders possession, the landlord can only obtain possession in a legal action for eviction. If successful, the landlord will be issued a *writ of possession* which the landlord will then request the local sheriff to serve on the tenant and, by evicting the tenant, hand possession of the property back to the landlord.

The landlord is prohibited by law in most states from 1) turning off the utilities for the property in an effort to force the tenant to move, 2) threatening or harassing the tenant in any way, 3) changing the locks or otherwise preventing the tenant from remaining in possession of the property. To reobtain possession of a property, the landlord must wait for surrender or abandonment, or take legal action for eviction. The use of many of the notices in this chapter however may indicate to a tenant in violation of the lease that the landlord is serious about enforceing the lease and is willing to pursue further legal action.

Notice of Rent Default: This form allows for notice to a tenant of default in the payment of rent. It provides for the amount of the defaulted payments to be specified and for a time limit to be placed on payment before further action is taken. Most states have laws relating to the time limits that must be allowed to a tenant to pay the late rent after the landlord's notice of a rent default. You should check your state's listing in the Appendix of this book for the time limit that you should use in this form. If the breach is not taken care of within the time period allowed, you may send the tenant a Notice to Pay Rent or Vacate (shown later in this chapter). In addition, a lawyer should be consulted for further action, which may involve a lawsuit to enforce the lease terms or for eviction. A copy of the original lease should be attached to this form.

To complete this form, fill in the following information:

① Date of notice
② Name of tenant
③ Address of tenant
④ Name of tenant
⑤ Description of lease (address of property, dates covered, etc.)
⑥ Date of this notice
⑦ Exact amount of rent past due
⑧ Number of days allowed to pay rent (Check the Appendix for your state's requirements)
⑨ Signature of landlord
⑩ Printed Name of landlord

Notice of Rent Default

Date: ① _____ , 20 ① _____

To: ②
    ③

RE: Notice of Rent Default

Dear ④ _____ :

This notice is in reference to the following described lease: ⑤

Please be advised that as of ⑥ _____ , 20 ⑥ _____ , you are in DEFAULT IN YOUR PAYMENT OF RENT in the amount of $ ⑦ _____ .

If this breach of lease is not corrected within ⑧ _____ days of this notice, we will take further action to protect our rights, which may include termination of this lease and collection proceedings. This notice is made under all applicable laws. All of our rights are reserved under this notice.

⑨ _____
Signature of Landlord

⑩ _____
Printed Name of Landlord

Notice of Breach of Lease: This form should be used to notify a party to a lease of the violation of a term of the lease or of an instance of failure to perform a required duty under the lease, other than the failure to pay rent. Such violation might be having a pet if the lease prohibits this, or perhaps having too many people living in the rental property, or any other violation of the terms of the lease. This notice provides for a description of the alleged violation of the lease and for a time period in which the party is instructed to cure the breach of the lease. If the breach is not taken care of within the time period allowed, you may send the tenant a Final Notice Before Legal Action. In any event, a lawyer should be consulted for further action, which may entail a lawsuit to enforce the lease terms or for eviction. A copy of the original lease should be attached to this form.

To complete this form, fill in the following information:

① Date of notice
② Name of tenant
③ Address of tenant
④ Name of tenant
⑤ Description of lease (address of property, dates covered, etc.)
⑥ Date of this notice
⑦ Exact description of breach of lease
⑧ Number of days allowed to correct the breach
⑨ Signature of landlord
⑩ Printed Name of landlord

Notice of Breach of Lease

Date: ①_____ , 20 ①_____

To: ②
    ③

RE: Breach of Lease

Dear ④_____ :

This notice is in reference to the following described lease: ⑤

Please be advised that as of ⑥_____ , 20 ⑥_____ , we are holding you in BREACH OF LEASE for the following reasons: ⑦

If this breach of lease is not corrected within ⑧_____ days of this notice, we will take further action to protect our rights, which may include termination of this lease. This notice is made under all applicable laws. All of our rights are reserved under this notice.

⑨
_____
Signature of Landlord

⑩
_____
Printed Name of Landlord

Notice of Intent to Enter: This form should be used to notify a tenant that a landlord intends to enter the leased property to take some type of action, such a repairing an appliance or for pest control or some other landlord duty. You should check the appendix for any state laws that may restrict a landlord's right to enter a leased property. You may use this form in conjunction with the Notice of Service Performed later in this chapter (which notifies the tenant that the landlord has completed performing some type of service to the rented property).

To complete this form, fill in the following information:

1. Date of notice
2. Name of tenant
3. Address of tenant
4. Name of tenant
5. Address of property
6. Date of intended entry into property
7. Time of intended entry into property
8. Reason for entry into property (such as: repair stove, pest control, etc.)
9. Signature of landlord
10. Printed Name of landlord

Notice of Intent to Enter

Date: ① _____ , 20 ① _____

To: ②
    ③

RE: Intent to Enter Property

Dear ④ _____ :

This notice is in reference to the following described property: ⑤

Please be advised that on ⑥ _____ , 20 ⑥ _____ , at approximately ⑦ _____ m. the landlord intends to enter the above property in order to perform the following service: ⑧

At such time, the landlord will use the master key for this property. Please have the property clean and presentable for the landlord's performance of this service. Thank you very much.

⑨ _____
Signature of Landlord

⑩ _____
Printed Name of Landlord

Notice to Pay Rent or Vacate: This form allows for notice to be given to a tenant who is in default of the payment of rent. It provides for the amount of the defaulted payments to be specified and for a time limit to be placed on payment before further action is taken. It provides notice to either pay the rent or to vacate the property by a certain date. If the defaulted rent is not paid or the property is not vacated by the tenant within the time period allowed, a Notice to Terminate Lease may be delivered to the tenant which demands that possession of the property be relinquished. Most states have laws relating to the time limits that must be allowed to a tenant to pay the late rent after the landlord's notice of a rent default. You should check your state's listing in the Appendix of this book for the time limit that you should use in this form. A lawyer should be consulted for further action, which may involve a lawsuit to enforce the lease terms, a lawsuit for collection of the past due rent, or legal proceedings for eviction of the tenant. A copy of the original lease should be attached to this form.

To complete this form, fill in the following information:

① Date of notice
② Name of tenant
③ Address of tenant
④ Name of tenant
⑤ Description of lease (address of property, dates covered, etc.)
⑥ Date of this notice
⑦ Exact amount of rent past due
⑧ Date on which tenant must pay rent or vacate the property (Check your state's listing in the Appendix)
⑨ Signature of landlord
⑩ Printed Name of landlord

Notice to Pay Rent or Vacate Property

Date: ① _____ , 20 ① _____

To: ②
③

RE: Notice to Vacate Property

Dear ④ _____ :

This notice is in reference to the following described lease: ⑤

Please be advised that as of ⑥ _____ , you are in DEFAULT OF YOUR PAYMENT OF RENT in the amount of $ ⑦ _____ , which is immediately payable.

THEREFORE, YOU ARE HEREBY GIVEN NOTICE:

To immediately pay the amount of rent that is in default as noted above or to immediately vacate the property and deliver possession to the Landlord on or before ⑧ _____ .
If you fail to pay the rent in default or vacate the property by this date, we will take further action to protect our rights, which may include termination of this lease, collection, and eviction proceedings. Be also advised that any legal costs involved in the collection of rent in default or in obtaining possession of this property will also be recovered from you as may be allowed by law. This notice is made under all applicable laws of this state. All of our rights are reserved under this notice. Regardless of your vacating the property, you are still responsible for all rent due under the lease.

THIS IS NOT AN EVICTION NOTICE.

⑨
_____
Signature of Landlord

⑩
_____
Printed Name of Landlord

Notice of Service Performed: By this notice, a landlord may inform a tenant that a certain service has been performed on the rented property, such as repairing an appliance or pest control, or some other landlord duty.

To complete this form, fill in the following information:

① Date of notice
② Name of tenant
③ Address of tenant
④ Name of tenant
⑤ Address of property
⑥ Date of performance of service
⑦ Time of performance of service
⑧ Type of service performed (such as: repair stove, pest control, etc.)
⑨ Signature of landlord
⑩ Printed Name of landlord

Notice of Service Performed

Date: ① _____ , 20 ① _____

To: ②
 ③

RE: Service Performed on Rental Property

Dear ④ _____ :

This notice is in reference to the following described property: ⑤

Please be advised that on ⑥ _____ , 20 ⑥ _____ , at approximately ⑦ _____ m. the following service was performed on the above property: ⑧

⑨ _____
Signature of Landlord

⑩ _____
Printed Name of Landlord

Notice to Terminate Lease: By this notice, a landlord may inform a tenant of the termination of a lease for breach of the lease. This action may be taken under a lease, provided that there are specific lease provisions that allow this action and the tenant has agreed to these provisions by signing the lease. This notice is generally sent to a tenant after the tenant has first been notified that the rent is past due or that the lease has been breached for other reasons and the tenant has been given a time period in which to pay. This notice is not an eviction notice. It is a notice to demand that the tenant surrender possession of the property back to the landlord. Some states have time limits that must be complied with before a lease can be terminated and you should check your state's listing in the Appendix to determine if your state has such requirements. A lawyer should be consulted for further action, which may involve a lawsuit to enforce the lease terms, a lawsuit for collection of the past-due rent, or legal proceedings for eviction of the tenant. A copy of the original lease should be attached to this form. This form should be delivered to the tenant by certified first-class mail and the Proof of Service portion of this form should be completed by the person actually mailing the notice.

To complete this form, fill in the following information:

1. Date of notice
2. Name and address of tenant
3. Name of tenant
4. Description of lease (address of property, dates covered, etc.)
5. Date of this Notice
6. Exact nature of breach of lease (amount rent past due, etc.)
7. Date of the original Notice to Pay Rent or Vacate or Notice of Breach of Lease
8. Number of days allowed in original Notice to Pay Rent or Vacate or Notice of Breach of Lease
9. Date on which possession of property is demanded
10. Signature of landlord
11. Printed Name of landlord
12. Address of landlord
13. City, state, and zip code of landlord
14. Date of mailing of Notice
15. Date of signature on Proof of Service
16. Signature of person mailing Notice
17. Printed name of person mailing Notice

Notice to Terminate Lease

Date: ① _____ , 20 ① _____

To: ②

RE: Notice to Terminate Lease

Dear ③ _____ :

This notice is in reference to the following described lease: ④

Please be advised that as of ⑤ _____ , 20 ⑤ _____ , you have been in BREACH
OF LEASE for the following reasons: ⑥

You were previously notified of this breach in the NOTICE dated ⑦ _____ ,
20 ⑦ _____ . At that time you were given ⑧ _____ days to correct the breach of
the lease and you have not complied.

THEREFORE, YOU ARE HEREBY GIVEN NOTICE:

The lease is immediately terminated and you are directed to deliver possession of the property
to the landlord on or before ⑨ _____ , 20 ⑨ _____ . If you fail to deliver the
property by this date, legal action to evict you from the property will be taken. Regardless of
your deliverance of the property, you are still responsible for all rent due under the lease.

⑩ _____
Signature of Landlord

⑪ _____
Printed Name of Landlord

⑫ _____
Address of Landlord

⑬ _____
City, State, Zip code of Landlord

PROOF OF SERVICE

I, the undersigned, being of legal age, declare under penalty of perjury that I served th
above Notice to Terminate Lease on the above-named tenant by mailing an exact copy to th
tenant by certified mail on ⑭ _____ .

Signed on: ⑮ _____

By: ⑯ _____
Signature of person mailing Notice

⑰ _____
Printed name of person mailing Notice

98

Final Notice Before Legal Action: This form allows for a final notice to be given to a person who is in default with a rent payment or other breach of a lease. It provides for the amount of the defaulted payments to be specified and for a time limit to be placed on payment before immediate legal action is taken. If the defaulted amount is not paid within the time period allowed, a lawyer should be consulted for further action, Further action may involve a lawsuit for collection of the past due amount, a lawsuit for possession of any collateral (if involved) or other legal proceedings. A copy of the original account statement or invoice should be attached to this form.

To complete this form, fill in the following information:

① Date of notice
② Name of person in default
③ Address of person in default
④ Description of lease which has been breached
⑤ Date of this notice
⑥ Exact amount of past due rent
⑦ Date on which payment must be made
⑧ Date of this notice
⑨ Signature of landlord
⑩ Printed name of landlord
⑪ Address of landlord
⑫ City, state, and zip code of landlord

Final Notice Before Legal Action

Date: ① _____ , 20 ① _____

To: ②
   ③

This notice is in reference to the following Lease: ④

Please be advised that as of ⑤ _____ , you are in DEFAULT ON THIS LEASE in the amount of $ ⑥ _____ , which is immediately due and payable. You have previously been repeatedly notified of your delinquency regarding this Lease.

THEREFORE, YOU ARE HEREBY GIVEN FINAL NOTICE:

That you must immediately pay the full amount that is in default as noted above on or before ⑦ _____ . If you fail to pay the full amount in default by this date, we will take immediate action to protect our rights by proceeding with legal action. Be also advised that any and all legal costs associated with such legal action will also be recovered from you to the fullest extent allowed by law and that such legal proceedings may impair your credit rating. This notice is made under all applicable laws of this state. All of our rights are reserved under this notice.

THIS IS YOUR FINAL OPPORTUNITY TO RESOLVE MATTERS WITHOUT THE EXPENSE OF COURT PROCEEDINGS.

Dated: ⑧ _____

⑨ _____
Signature of Landlord

⑩ _____
Printed Name of Landlord

⑪ _____
Address

⑫ _____
City, State, Zip Code

100

Notice of Approval of Tenant Alterations to Property: This notice is provided to give permission to a tenant to make alterations to the leased property. All of the leases in this book require that a tenant obtain permission of the landlord prior to making any alterations to the property. With this notice, the landlord can provide a written statement regarding the exact extent to the allowed alterations for which permission has been granted.

To complete this form, fill in the following information:

① Date of notice
② Name of tenant
③ Address of tenant
④ Name of tenant
⑤ Address of property
⑥ Date of intended alterations to property
⑦ Complete description of alterations to property for which permission is granted
⑧ Signature of landlord
⑨ Printed Name of landlord

Notice of Approval of Tenant Alterations to Property

Date: ① _____ , 20 ① ____

To: ②
    ③

RE: Permission to Alter Rental Property

Dear ④ _____ :

This notice is in reference to the following described property: ⑤

Please be advised that on ⑥ _____ , 20 ⑥ ____ , Landlord has approved the following
tenant alterations to the above property: ⑦

Tenant must perform all such permitted alterations in a workmanlike manner and keep the
premises clean and sanitary throughout the alteration period.

⑧ _____
Signature of Landlord

⑨ _____
Printed Name of Landlord

Notice of Lease: This document should be used to record notice that a parcel of real estate has a current lease in effect on it. This may be necessary if the property is on the market for sale or it may be required by a bank or mortgage company at the closing of a real estate sale in order for the seller to verify to the buyer the existence of a lease covering the property. This form should be notarized.

In order to complete this document, the following information is required:

① Description of lease
② Name of landlord
③ Address of landlord
④ Name of tenant
⑤ Address of tenant
⑥ Description of property leased
⑦ Term of lease
⑧ Any extensions of lease
⑨ Signature of landlord
⑩ Printed name of landlord

The following should be completed by a notary public:

⑪ State where document is notarized
⑫ County where document is notarized
⑬ Date when notarized
⑭ Name of Landlord
⑮ Signature of Notary
⑯ County where document is notarized
⑰ State where document is notarized
⑱ Expiration date of Notary Public's commission
⑲ Official Seal of Notary Public

Notice of Lease

NOTICE is given of the existence of the following lease: ①

Name of landlord: ②
Address: ③

Name of tenant: ④
Address: ⑤

Description of property leased: ⑥

Term of lease: From ⑦ _____ , 20 ⑦ ____ , to ⑦ _____ , 20 ⑦ ____ .

Any options to extend lease: ⑧

⑨ _____
Signature of Landlord

⑩ _____
Printed Name of Landlord

State of ⑪ _____
County of ⑫ _____

On ⑬ _____ , 20 ⑬ ____ , ⑭ _____
personally came before me and, being duly sworn, did state that he or she is the person described in the above document and that he or she signed the above document in my presence.

⑮ _____
Signature of Notary Public

Notary Public, In and for the County of ⑯ _____
State of ⑰ _____

My commission expires: ⑱ _____   Notary Seal ⑲

CHAPTER 5
Additional Landlord Forms

Rental Application: This form is the basis of a check into the credit history and/or references of a potential tenant. With this form, an applicant furnishes various information which may be checked further to ascertain the reliability and background of the tenant applicant. The applicant is requested to furnish personal information, two credit references, two bank references, two landlord references, and answer a few basic questions. The form also provides for information to be entered regarding the verification of the references. If a rental applicant is denied, a Notice of Denial of Rental Application should be sent to the applicant. This form is explained later in this chapter.

The Applicant will furnish the following information:

1. Name, address, phone number, fax number, and e-mail address of applicant
2. Creditor #1- Name, account number, phone, and address of creditor #1
3. Creditor #2- Name, account number, phone, and address of creditor #2
4. Bank #1- Name, account number, phone, and address of bank #1
5. Bank #2- Name, account number, phone, and address of bank #2
6. Landlord Reference #1- Name, address of rental, phone, and address of landlord #1
7. Landlord Reference #2- Name, address of rental, phone, and address of landlord #2
8. Other informations (bankruptcy, felony, eviction, etc.)
9. Applicant's driver's license number and state issuing driver's license
10. Date of Application
11. Signature of Applicant
12. Printed Name of Applicant

Landlord to fill in the following information:

13. Person at Credit reference #1 contacted
14. Remarks
15. Person at Credit reference #2 contacted
16. Remarks
17. Person at Bank reference #1 contacted
18. Remarks
19. Person at Bank reference #2 contacted
20. Remarks
21. Landlord reference #1 contacted
22. Remarks

㉓ Landlord reference #2 contacted
㉔ Remarks
㉕ Person contacting references
㉖ Date references contacted
㉗ Applicant approval
㉘ Person making approval
㉙ Date of approval
㉚ Person making denial
㉛ Date of denial
㉜ Reason for denial
㉝ Has notice of denial been sent?

Rental Application

Name   ①
Address
City
State   Zip
Phone
Fax
e-mail Address

CREDIT REFERENCES

Creditor Name   ②
Account Number
Phone
Address
City
State   Zip

Creditor Name   ③
Account Number
Phone
Address
City
State   Zip

BANK REFERENCES

Bank Name   ④
Account Number
Phone
Address
City
State   Zip

Bank Name   ⑤
Account Number
Phone
Address
City
State   Zip

LANDLORD REFERENCES
Name   ⑥
Address of Rental
Phone
Address of Landlord
City
State   Zip

Name   ⑦
Address of Rental
Phone
Address of Landlord
City
State   Zip

OTHER INFORMATION
Have you ever filed for bankruptcy? **YES / NO** ⑧
Have you ever been convicted of a felony? **YES / NO** ⑧
Have you ever been evicted from or asked to leave a property you were renting? **YES / NO** ⑧
Have you ever intentionally refused to pay rent when due? **YES / NO** ⑧
How were you referred to us? ⑧
Driver's License Number: ⑨   State: ⑨

The Applicant accepts the above terms and states that all information contained in this application is true and correct. Applicant authorizes the landlord to contact all references and prior landlords, inquire as to credit information, and receive any confidential information relevant to approving this application.

Dated: ⑩ _____

⑪ _____
Signature of Applicant

⑫ _____
Printed Name of Applicant

References Contacted	Person Contacted	Remarks
Creditor #1	⑬	⑭
Creditor #2	⑮	⑯
Bank #1	⑰	⑱
Bank #2	⑲	⑳
Landlord #1	㉑	㉒
Landlord #2	㉓	㉔

References Contacted by: ㉕
Date References Contacted: ㉖

Applicant Approved: **YES / NO** ㉗
Approval by: ㉘
Date Approved: ㉙
Denial by: ㉚
Date Denied: ㉛
Reason for Denial ㉜
Denial Notice Sent: **YES / NO** ㉝

Notice of Denial of Rental Application: By this notice, a landlord may inform a rental applicant that their application for rental has been denied. A landlord should develop a system by which to grade the rental applications so that each prospective tenant is evaluated in the same manner. Such evaluation may be based only on non-discriminatory factors. Denial of a prospective tenant may not be based on the tenant's race, disability, religion, color, creed, ethnic origin, or age (if the applicant is over the age of 40). In addition, some localities also prohibit discrimination based on one's occupation or sexual orientation. This notice provides a clear explanation to a tenant regarding the specific reasons that the application was denied. This notice also provides the required notice to the tenant of his or her rights under the Fair Credit Reporting Act, as amended by the Fair and Accurate Credit Transactions Act of 2003 (15 USC 1681).

To complete this form, fill in the following information:

① Date of notice
② Name and address of tenant
③ Name of tenant
④ Description of property
⑤ Checkmark before reason for denial of application (Note: If the denial was based on an insufficient or negative credit report, you must supply the name, address, and phone number for the credit agency which provided the report that was relied upon to deny the application)
⑥ Signature of landlord
⑦ Printed Name of landlord

Notice of Denial of Rental Application

Date: ① _____ , 20 ① _____

To: ②

RE: Notice Denial of Rental Application

Dear ③ _____ :

This notice is in reference to the following property: ④

Please be advised that your application to rent the above property has been denied for the following reasons:

⑤   ☐ Insufficient information in credit report
      Name, address, and phone number of credit reporting agency (Toll-free number must be provided if agency was a national credit reporting agency:_____

_____

⑤   ☐ Negative information in credit report
      Name, address, and phone number of credit reporting agency (Toll-free number must be provided if agency was a national credit reporting agency:_____

_____

⑤   ☐ Unable to verify and/or obtain positive references
⑤   ☐ Unable to verify and/or obtain positive recommendations from prior landlords
⑤   ☐ Earlier applicant

⑥ _____
Signature of Landlord

⑦ _____
Printed Name of Landlord

You have the right under the federal Fair Credit Reporting Act, as amended by the Fair and Accurate Credit Transactions Act of 2003 (15 USC 1681), to obtain a free copy of your credit report from the consumer credit agency named above if your request is made within 60 days of this notice and if you have not requested a free copy within the past year (15 USC 1681j). You also have the right to dispute the accuracy or completeness of your credit report and add your own "consumer statement" of up to 100 words to the report (15 USC 1681i). For more information, contact the credit agency listed above.

Receipt for Lease Security Deposit: This form is to be used for receipt of a lease security deposit. To complete this form, insert the following information:

① Amount of security deposit paid
② Description of lease
③ Date of receipt
④ Signature of landlord
⑤ Printed name of landlord

Receipt for Lease Security Deposit

The landlord acknowledges receipt of the sum of $ ① _____ paid by the tenant under the following described lease: ②

This security deposit payment will be held by the landlord under the terms of this lease, and unless required by law, will not bear any interest and will not be held in a separate trust account. This security deposit will be repaid when due under the terms of the lease, less any reasonable deductions for repair and/or cleaning and/or unpaid rent.

Dated: ③ _____ , 20 ③ ____

④ _____
Signature of Landlord

⑤ _____
Printed Name of Landlord

Lease Security Deposit Return Letter: This letter is used to return a tenant's security deposit and, if necessary, explain the reasons for any deductions from the deposit.

To complete this form, fill in the following information:

① Date of notice
② Name and address of tenant
③ Name of tenant
④ Description of lease (address of property, dates covered, etc.)
⑤ Date of this Notice
⑥ Date of end of lease
⑦ Amount of initial security deposit
⑧ Amount of any required interest on security deposit
⑨ Amount of total security deposit (including interest)
⑩ Details and amount of any deductions for necessary repairs
⑪ Details and amount of any deductions for necessary cleaning
⑫ Details and amount of any deductions for any unpaid rent
⑬ Total amount of deductions from security deposit
⑭ Total amount of security deposit to be returned (Enclose check for this amount)
⑮ Signature of landlord
⑯ Printed Name of landlord

Lease Security Deposit Return Letter

Date: ① _____ , 20 ① ____

To: ②

RE: Return of Security Deposit

Dear ③ _____ :

This notice is in reference to the following described lease: ④

On ⑤ _____ , 20 ⑤ ____ , you provided a rental security deposit under the terms of the above lease. That lease ended on ⑥ _____ , 20 ⑥ ____ , and, under the terms of the lease, your security deposit is being returned, less any deductions for necessary repairs (beyond normal wear and tear), and/or cleaning of the property, and/or unpaid rent. If interest was required to be paid on this security deposit, it is also noted. The following is the disposition of your security deposit:

Amount of initial security deposit: $ ⑦ _____
Amount of any required interest: $ ⑧ _____
Total security deposit: $ ⑨ _____
Less deductions for necessary repairs:
    Details: ⑩ _____
    $ ⑩ _____
Less deductions for necessary cleaning:
    Details: ⑪ _____
    $ ⑪ _____
Less deductions for unpaid rent:
    Details: ⑫ _____
    $ ⑫ _____
Total deductions: $ ⑬ _____
Remaining security deposit being returned: $ ⑭ _____

Enclosed please find a check in that amount (if applicable). Thank you.

⑮ _____
Signature of Landlord

⑯ _____
Printed Name of Landlord

Rent Receipt: This form may be used as a receipt for the periodic payment of rent. To complete this form, insert the following information:

① Amount of rent paid
② Name of Tenant
③ Time period
④ Description of property for which rent is due
⑤ Date of receipt
⑥ Signature of landlord
⑦ Printed Name of landlord

Rent Receipt

The landlord acknowledges receipt of the sum of $ ① _____ paid by
② _____ , the tenant, for rent
during the time period of ③ _____ to ③ _____ for the
property located at: ④ _____ .

Dated: ⑤ _____ , 20 ⑤ ____

⑥ _____   ⑦ _____
Signature of Landlord   Printed Name of Landlord

Move-in/Move-out Checklist and Acknowledgment: This form is to be used to catalog and note the condition of all of the furniture, furnishings, appliances, and personal property that are present at the leased property. The tenant is responsible for returning all of the following property in as good a condition as is noted on the Move-in section of this form, except for normal wear and tear. Landlord should complete this form prior to move-in and Tenant should check this form upon move-in, noting any disagreements with landlord's assessment. Both Tenant and Landlord should sign the form at move-in. When the Tenant moves out, the Landlord should again check the presence and condition of the items listed on this form and note the condition of such items on the form. The Tenant should then check the items and note any disagreements with the Landlord's assessment of the condition or presence of any of the items listed. Both the Tenant and Landlord should sign this form again at the moving out of the Tenant. This form may be used to determine any deductions from the security deposit of the Tenant. Both the Landlord and the Tenant should get a copy of this form. To complete this form, enter the following information:

①　Name of landlord
②　Name of tenant
③　Address of leased property
④　Term of the lease
⑤　Date tenant moves into property
⑥　Date tenant moves out of property
⑦　Listing of all items and their condition (Complete at time of move-in and again at time of move-out)
⑧　Date of landlord signature for move-in condition
⑨　Signature of landlord for move-in condition
⑩　Date of tenant signature for move-in condition
⑪　Signature of tenant for move-in condition
⑫　Date of landlord signature for move-out condition
⑬　Signature of landlord for move-out condition
⑭　Date of tenant signature for move-out condition
⑮　Signature of tenant for move-out condition

Move In/Move Out Checklist and Acknowledgment

Landlord Name: ①

Tenant Name: ②

Address of leased property: ③

Term of Lease: ④

Date of Move-in: ⑤

Date of Move-out: ⑥

This form is to catalog and note the condition of all of the furniture, furnishing, appliances, and personal property that is present at the leased property. The tenant is responsible for returning all of the following property upon moving out in as good a condition as is noted on the Move-in section of this form, except for normal wear and tear. Landlord should complete this form prior to move-in and Tenant should check this form upon move-in, noting any disagreements with landlord's assessment.

Item Description	Move-in Condition	Landlord Comments	Tenant Comments	Move-out Condition	Landlord Comments	Tenant Comments
⑦						

Move-in Acknowledgment

Landlord has reviewed this document and agrees with the items listed and their condition on the date of the Tenant's moving into the leased property.

Date: ⑧ _____

⑨ _____
Landlord Signature

Tenant has inspected all of the listed items and found them to be present on the leased property and to be in the condition indicated on the date of the Tenant's moving in to the leased property (or else has noted any discrepancy on this form). Tenant agrees to return all of the listed property on the date of moving out of the leased property in the same condition as indicated on this form, except for normal wear and tear. By signing this form, Tenant agrees with Landlord's assessment or notes his or her disagreement with the Landlord.

Date: ⑩ _____

⑪ _____
Tenant Signature

Move-out Acknowledgment

Landlord has inspected the listed items and compared them to the move-in condition. If any property differs from its move-in condition, other than normal wear and tear, any differences have been listed on this form.

Date: ⑫ _____

⑬ _____
Landlord Signature

Tenant has inspected the listed items and compared them to the move-in condition. If any property differs from its move-in condition, other than normal wear and tear, any differences have been listed on this form. If Tenant disagrees with Landlord's assessment of any differences in condition upon moving out, those discrepancies have been listed on this form. By signing this form, Tenant agrees with Landlord's assessment or notes his or her disagreement with the Landlord.

Date: ⑭ _____

⑮ _____
Tenant Signature

Protect Your Family From Lead In Your Home

EPA United States Environmental Protection Agency

United States Consumer Product Safety Commission

United States Department of Housing and Urban Development

Are You Planning To Buy, Rent, or Renovate a Home Built Before 1978?

Many houses and apartments built before 1978 have paint that contains high levels of lead (called lead-based paint). Lead from paint, chips, and dust can pose serious health hazards if not taken care of properly.

OWNERS, BUYERS, and RENTERS are encouraged to check for lead (see page 6) before renting, buying or renovating pre-1978 housing.

Federal law requires that individuals receive certain information before renting, buying, or renovating pre-1978 housing:

LANDLORDS have to disclose known information on lead-based paint and lead-based paint hazards before leases take effect. Leases must include a disclosure about lead-based paint.

SELLERS have to disclose known information on lead-based paint and lead-based paint hazards before selling a house. Sales contracts must include a disclosure about lead-based paint. Buyers have up to 10 days to check for lead.

RENOVATORS disturbing more than 2 square feet of painted surfaces have to give you this pamphlet before starting work.

IMPORTANT!

Lead From Paint, Dust, and Soil Can Be Dangerous If Not Managed Properly

FACT: Lead exposure can harm young children and babies even before they are born.

FACT: Even children who seem healthy can have high levels of lead in their bodies.

FACT: People can get lead in their bodies by breathing or swallowing lead dust, or by eating soil or paint chips containing lead.

FACT: People have many options for reducing lead hazards. In most cases, lead-based paint that is in good condition is not a hazard.

FACT: Removing lead-based paint improperly can increase the danger to your family.

If you think your home might have lead hazards, read this pamphlet to learn some simple steps to protect your family.

Lead Gets in the Body in Many Ways

Childhood lead poisoning remains a major environmental health problem in the U.S.

Even children who appear healthy can have dangerous levels of lead in their bodies.

People can get lead in their body if they:

Breathe in lead dust (especially during renovations that disturb painted surfaces).

Put their hands or other objects covered with lead dust in their mouths.

Eat paint chips or soil that contains lead.

Lead is even more dangerous to children under the age of 6:

At this age children's brains and nervous systems are more sensitive to the damaging effects of lead.

Children's growing bodies absorb more lead.

Babies and young children often put their hands and other objects in their mouths. These objects can have lead dust on them.

Lead is also dangerous to women of childbearing age:

Women with a high lead level in their system prior to pregnancy would expose a fetus to lead through the placenta during fetal development.

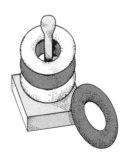

1

2

Lead's Effects

It is important to know that even exposure to low levels of lead can severely harm children.

In children, lead can cause:

Nervous system and kidney damage.

Learning disabilities, attention deficit disorder, and decreased intelligence.

Speech, language, and behavior problems.

Poor muscle coordination.

Decreased muscle and bone growth.

Hearing damage.

While low-lead exposure is most common, exposure to high levels of lead can have devastating effects on children, including seizures, unconsciousness, and, in some cases, death.

Although children are especially susceptible to lead exposure, lead can be dangerous for adults too.

In adults, lead can cause:

Increased chance of illness during pregnancy.

Harm to a fetus, including brain damage or death.

Fertility problems (in men and women).

High blood pressure.

Digestive problems.

Nerve disorders.

Memory and concentration problems.

Muscle and joint pain.

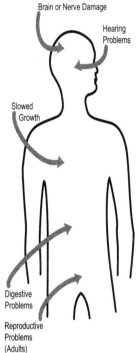

Brain or Nerve Damage

Hearing Problems

Slowed Growth

Digestive Problems

Reproductive Problems (Adults)

Lead affects the body in many ways.

3

Where Lead-Based Paint Is Found

In general, the older your home, the more likely it has lead-based paint.

Many homes built before 1978 have lead-based paint. The federal government banned lead-based paint from housing in 1978. Some states stopped its use even earlier. Lead can be found:

In homes in the city, country, or suburbs.

In apartments, single-family homes, and both private and public housing.

Inside and outside of the house.

In soil around a home. (Soil can pick up lead from exterior paint or other sources such as past use of leaded gas in cars.)

Checking Your Family for Lead

Get your children and home tested if you think your home has high levels of lead.

To reduce your child's exposure to lead, get your child checked, have your home tested (especially if your home has paint in poor condition and was built before 1978), and fix any hazards you may have. Children's blood lead levels tend to increase rapidly from 6 to 12 months of age, and tend to peak at 18 to 24 months of age.

Consult your doctor for advice on testing your children. A simple blood test can detect high levels of lead. Blood tests are usually recommended for:

Children at ages 1 and 2.

Children or other family members who have been exposed to high levels of lead.

Children who should be tested under your state or local health screening plan.

Your doctor can explain what the test results mean and if more testing will be needed.

4

Identifying Lead Hazards

Lead-based paint is usually not a hazard if it is in good condition, and it is not on an impact or friction surface, like a window. It is defined by the federal government as paint with lead levels greater than or equal to 1.0 milligram per square centimeter, or more than 0.5% by weight.

Deteriorating lead-based paint (peeling, chipping, chalking, cracking or damaged) is a hazard and needs immediate attention. It may also be a hazard when found on surfaces that children can chew or that get a lot of wear-and-tear, such as:

Windows and window sills.

Doors and door frames.

Stairs, railings, banisters, and porches.

Lead dust can form when lead-based paint is scraped, sanded, or heated. Dust also forms when painted surfaces bump or rub together. Lead chips and dust can get on surfaces and objects that people touch. Settled lead dust can re-enter the air when people vacuum, sweep, or walk through it. The following two federal standards have been set for lead hazards in dust:

40 micrograms per square foot ($\mu g/ft^2$) and higher for floors, including carpeted floors.

250 $\mu g/ft^2$ and higher for interior window sills.

Lead in soil can be a hazard when children play in bare soil or when people bring soil into the house on their shoes. The following two federal standards have been set for lead hazards in residential soil:

400 parts per million (ppm) and higher in play areas of bare soil.

1,200 ppm (average) and higher in bare soil in the remainder of the yard.

The only way to find out if paint, dust and soil lead hazards exist is to test for them. The next page describes the most common methods used.

> **Lead from paint chips, which you can see, and lead dust, which you can't always see, can both be serious hazards.**

5

Checking Your Home for Lead

> **Just knowing that a home has lead-based paint may not tell you if there is a hazard.**

You can get your home tested for lead in several different ways:

A paint **inspection** tells you whether your home has lead-based paint and where it is located. It won't tell you whether or not your home currently has lead hazards.

A **risk assessment** tells you if your home currently has any lead hazards from lead in paint, dust, or soil. It also tells you what actions to take to address any hazards.

A combination risk assessment and inspection tells you if your home has any lead hazards and if your home has any lead-based paint, and where the lead-based paint is located.

Hire a trained and certified testing professional who will use a range of reliable methods when testing your home.

Visual inspection of paint condition and location.

A portable x-ray fluorescence (XRF) machine.

Lab tests of paint, dust, and soil samples.

There are state and federal programs in place to ensure that testing is done safely, reliably, and effectively. Contact your state or local agency (see bottom of page 11) for more information, or call **1-800-424-LEAD (5323)** for a list of contacts in your area.

Home test kits for lead are available, but may not always be accurate. Consumers should not rely on these kits before doing renovations or to assure safety.

6

What You Can Do Now To Protect Your Family

If you suspect that your house has lead hazards, you can take some immediate steps to reduce your family's risk:

If you rent, notify your landlord of peeling or chipping paint.

Clean up paint chips immediately.

Clean floors, window frames, window sills, and other surfaces weekly. Use a mop or sponge with warm water and a general all-purpose cleaner or a cleaner made specifically for lead. REMEMBER: NEVER MIX AMMONIA AND BLEACH PRODUCTS TOGETHER SINCE THEY CAN FORM A DANGEROUS GAS.

Thoroughly rinse sponges and mop heads after cleaning dirty or dusty areas.

Wash children's hands often, especially before they eat and before nap time and bed time.

Keep play areas clean. Wash bottles, pacifiers, toys, and stuffed animals regularly.

Keep children from chewing window sills or other painted surfaces.

Clean or remove shoes before entering your home to avoid tracking in lead from soil.

Make sure children eat nutritious, low-fat meals high in iron and calcium, such as spinach and dairy products. Children with good diets absorb less lead.

7

Reducing Lead Hazards In The Home

Removing lead improperly can increase the hazard to your family by spreading even more lead dust around the house.

Always use a professional who is trained to remove lead hazards safely.

In addition to day-to-day cleaning and good nutrition:

You can **temporarily** reduce lead hazards by taking actions such as repairing damaged painted surfaces and planting grass to cover soil with high lead levels. These actions (called "interim controls") are not permanent solutions and will need ongoing attention.

To **permanently** remove lead hazards, you should hire a certified lead "abatement" contractor. Abatement (or permanent hazard elimination) methods include removing, sealing, or enclosing lead-based paint with special materials. Just painting over the hazard with regular paint is not permanent removal.

Always hire a person with special training for correcting lead problems—someone who knows how to do this work safely and has the proper equipment to clean up thoroughly. Certified contractors will employ qualified workers and follow strict safety rules as set by their state or by the federal government.

Once the work is completed, dust cleanup activities must be repeated until testing indicates that lead dust levels are below the following:

40 micrograms per square foot ($\mu g/ft^2$) for floors, including carpeted floors;

250 $\mu g/ft^2$ for interior windows sills; and

400 $\mu g/ft^2$ for window troughs.

Call your state or local agency (see bottom of page 11) for help in locating certified professionals in your area and to see if financial assistance is available.

8

Remodeling or Renovating a Home With Lead-Based Paint

Take precautions before your contractor or you begin remodeling or renovating anything that disturbs painted surfaces (such as scraping off paint or tearing out walls):

Have the area tested for lead-based paint.

Do not use a belt-sander, propane torch, high temperature heat gun, dry scraper, or dry sandpaper to remove lead-based paint. These actions create large amounts of lead dust and fumes. Lead dust can remain in your home long after the work is done.

Temporarily move your family (especially children and pregnant women) out of the apartment or house until the work is done and the area is properly cleaned. If you can't move your family, at least completely seal off the work area.

Follow other safety measures to reduce lead hazards. You can find out about other safety measures by calling 1-800-424-LEAD. Ask for the brochure "Reducing Lead Hazards When Remodeling Your Home." This brochure explains what to do before, during, and after renovations.

If you have already completed renovations or remodeling that could have released lead-based paint or dust, get your young children tested and follow the steps outlined on page 7 of this brochure.

If not conducted properly, certain types of renovations can release lead from paint and dust into the air.

Other Sources of Lead

While paint, dust, and soil are the most common sources of lead, other lead sources also exist.

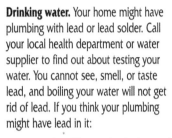

Drinking water. Your home might have plumbing with lead or lead solder. Call your local health department or water supplier to find out about testing your water. You cannot see, smell, or taste lead, and boiling your water will not get rid of lead. If you think your plumbing might have lead in it:

• Use only cold water for drinking and cooking.

• Run water for 15 to 30 seconds before drinking it, especially if you have not used your water for a few hours.

The job. If you work with lead, you could bring it home on your hands or clothes. Shower and change clothes before coming home. Launder your work clothes separately from the rest of your family's clothes.

Old painted **toys** and **furniture.**

Food and liquids stored in **lead crystal** or **lead-glazed pottery or porcelain.**

Lead smelters or other industries that release lead into the air.

Hobbies that use lead, such as making pottery or stained glass, or refinishing furniture.

Folk remedies that contain lead, such as "greta" and "azarcon" used to treat an upset stomach.

9   10

For More Information

The National Lead Information Center

Call **1-800-424-LEAD (424-5323)** to learn how to protect children from lead poisoning and for other information on lead hazards. To access lead information via the web, visit **www.epa.gov/lead** and **www.hud.gov/offices/lead/**.

EPA's Safe Drinking Water Hotline

Call **1-800-426-4791** for information about lead in drinking water.

Consumer Product Safety Commission (CPSC) Hotline

To request information on lead in consumer products, or to report an unsafe consumer product or a product-related injury call **1-800-638-2772**, or visit CPSC's Web site at: **www.cpsc.gov.**

Health and Environmental Agencies

Some cities, states, and tribes have their own rules for lead-based paint activities. Check with your local agency to see which laws apply to you. Most agencies can also provide information on finding a lead abatement firm in your area, and on possible sources of financial aid for reducing lead hazards. Receive up-to-date address and phone information for your local contacts on the Internet at **www.epa.gov/lead** or contact the National Lead Information Center at **1-800-424-LEAD.**

For the hearing impaired, call the Federal Information Relay Service at **1-800-877-8339** to access any of the phone numbers in this brochure.

11

EPA Regional Offices

Your Regional EPA Office can provide further information regarding regulations and lead protection programs.

EPA Regional Offices

Region 1 (Connecticut, Massachusetts, Maine, New Hampshire, Rhode Island, Vermont)

Regional Lead Contact
U.S. EPA Region 1
Suite 1100 (CPT)
One Congress Street
Boston, MA 02114-2023
1 (888) 372-7341

Region 2 (New Jersey, New York, Puerto Rico, Virgin Islands)

Regional Lead Contact
U.S. EPA Region 2
2890 Woodbridge Avenue
Building 209, Mail Stop 225
Edison, NJ 08837-3679
(732) 321-6671

Region 3 (Delaware, Maryland, Pennsylvania, Virginia, Washington DC, West Virginia)

Regional Lead Contact
U.S. EPA Region 3 (3WC33)
1650 Arch Street
Philadelphia, PA 19103
(215) 814-5000

Region 4 (Alabama, Florida, Georgia, Kentucky, Mississippi, North Carolina, South Carolina, Tennessee)

Regional Lead Contact
U.S. EPA Region 4
61 Forsyth Street, SW
Atlanta, GA 30303
(404) 562-8998

Region 5 (Illinois, Indiana, Michigan, Minnesota, Ohio, Wisconsin)

Regional Lead Contact
U.S. EPA Region 5 (DT-8J)
77 West Jackson Boulevard
Chicago, IL 60604-3666
(312) 886-6003

Region 6 (Arkansas, Louisiana, New Mexico, Oklahoma, Texas)

Regional Lead Contact
U.S. EPA Region 6
1445 Ross Avenue, 12th Floor
Dallas, TX 75202-2733
(214) 665-7577

Region 7 (Iowa, Kansas, Missouri, Nebraska)

Regional Lead Contact
U.S. EPA Region 7
(ARTD-RALI)
901 N. 5th Street
Kansas City, KS 66101
(913) 551-7020

Region 8 (Colorado, Montana, North Dakota, South Dakota, Utah, Wyoming)

Regional Lead Contact
U.S. EPA Region 8
999 18th Street, Suite 500
Denver, CO 80202-2466
(303) 312-6021

Region 9 (Arizona, California, Hawaii, Nevada)

Regional Lead Contact
U.S. Region 9
75 Hawthorne Street
San Francisco, CA 94105
(415) 947-4164

Region 10 (Alaska, Idaho, Oregon, Washington)

Regional Lead Contact
U.S. EPA Region 10
Toxics Section WCM-128
1200 Sixth Avenue
Seattle, WA 98101-1128
(206) 553-1985

12

CPSC Regional Offices

Your Regional CPSC Office can provide further information regarding regulations and consumer product safety.

Eastern Regional Center
Consumer Product Safety Commission
201 Varick Street, Room 903
New York, NY 10014
(212) 620-4120

Western Regional Center
Consumer Product Safety Commission
1301 Clay Street, Suite 610-N
Oakland, CA 94612
(510) 637-4050

Central Regional Center
Consumer Product Safety Commission
230 South Dearborn Street, Room 2944
Chicago, IL 60604
(312) 353-8260

HUD Lead Office

Please contact HUD's Office of Healthy Homes and Lead Hazard Control for information on lead regulations, outreach efforts, and lead hazard control and research grant programs.

U.S. Department of Housing and Urban Development
Office of Healthy Homes and Lead Hazard Control
451 Seventh Street, SW, P-3206
Washington, DC 20410
(202) 755-1785

U.S. EPA Washington DC 20460
U.S. CPSC Washington DC 20207
U.S. HUD Washington DC 20410

EPA747-K-99-001
June 2003

13

Appendix:
State Landlord/Tenant Laws

On the following pages are state listings containing relevant information regarding real estate and landlord/tenant law. You are advised to check your state's listing carefully to determine the particular requirements in your jurisdiction. Every state has some differing requirements. Following is an explanation of the listings:

State Landlord-Tenant Statutes: This listing provides a reference to the statute book location that contains each particular state's laws regarding landlord/tenant relations.

State Property Law Statutes: Should you wish to research the law in your state, this lists the name and chapter of the state statute in which the laws regarding real property are found in each state.

State web address: This listing notes the internet web address of each state's online website. For most state sites, you will arrive at the main index for the state and will need to locate the specific site for the state's statute/legislative information by using the references in the listings above, *State Landlord-Tenant Statutes* and *State Property Law Statutes*. These websites were current at the time of this book's publication.

State Real Estate Disclosure Laws: This listing specifies the name of the document that is required to be completed by a seller disclosing their knowledge about the property for sale. At press time, 31 states provided some type of statutory real estate disclosure form. A few states also require certain disclosures by landlords relating to rental property. These are also noted. Also noted is the statutory location of real estate disclosure laws. Please also note that this is one of the most rapidly changing areas of property law. You are advised to check locally to see if any other landlord disclosures are required.

Landlord's Entry to Real Estate: This listing provides the state requirement surrounding the right of a landlord to enter a rented property.

Security Deposit Amount Limits: Under this listing are noted the various state limits on the amount that a tenant can be charged as a security deposit.

Deadlines for Security Deposit Returns: Details are provided under this listing regarding the time limits imposed by each state for the return of a tenant's security deposit.

Interest Required on Security Deposits: This listing provides each state's requirements regarding whether a landlord must provide interest to the tenant for the holding period of the tenant's security deposit.

Separate Account Required for Security Deposits: This listing specifies whether a landlord is required to keep tenant security deposits in a separate bank account.

Additional Security Deposit Language in Lease: Under this listing are noted any additional language that is required in a residential lease relating to security deposits. Only 9 states require additional language (Alaska, Florida, Georgia, Kentucky, Maryland, Michigan, North Carolina, Tennessee, and Washington.

Exemption from Security Deposit Laws: This listing specifies which, if any, rental units are exempt from security deposit laws.

Notice Required to Change or Terminate Month-to-Month Tenancy: This listing provides the time limit required of a landlord to provide a tenant with notice that a month-to-month tenancy is being changed or terminated.

Number of Days for Pay Rent or Vacate Notice: This listing provides the minimum number of days that must be afforded to a tenant to bring their late rent up to date in a Notice to Pay Rent or Vacate.

Rent Late Fees: This listing provides state requirements surrounding the ability of a landlord to impose fees for the late payment of rent and any restrictions as to the amount of those fees.

Alabama

State Landlord-Tenant Statutes: The Code of Alabama, Sections 35-9-1 to 35-9-100.

State Property Laws Statutes: The Code of Alabama, Title 35.

State Law Website: www.legislature.state.al.us/CodeofAlabama/1975/coatoc.htm

State Real Estate Disclosure Laws: No statutory form.

Landlord's Entry to Real Estate: No statute.

Security Deposit Amount Limits: No statute.

Deadlines for Security Deposit Returns: No statute.

Interest Required on Security Deposit: No statute.

Separate Account required for Security Deposit: No statute.

Additional Security Deposit Language in Lease: None.

Exemption from Security Deposit Laws: No statute.

Notice Required to Change or Terminate Month-to-Month Tenancy: 10 days to terminate. No statute to change rent. (The Code of Alabama, Section 35-9-3).

Number of Days for Pay Rent or Vacate Notice: 10 days.

Rent Late Fees: No statute.

Alaska

State Landlord-Tenant Statutes: Alaska Statutes, Sections 34.03.010 to 34.03.380.

State Property Laws Statutes: Alaska Statutes, Title 34.

State Law Website: www.touchngo.com/lglcntr/akstats/Statutes.htm

State Real Estate Disclosure Laws: Residential Real Property Transfer Disclosure Statement. (Alaska Statutes, Title 34, Chapter 70). Disclosures in Residential Real Property Transfers. These forms are only necessary for the sale of real estate.

Landlord's Entry to Real Estate: Immediate access for emergency. 24 hour notice for inspection, repairs, viewing of property and if tenant is absent for long periods. (Alaska Statutes, Section 34.03.140).

Security Deposit Amount Limits: 2 months rent. (Alaska Statutes, Section 34.03.070).

Deadlines for Security Deposit Returns: 14 days if the tenant gives proper notice to terminate rent. 30 days if tenant does not give proper notice. (Alaska Statutes, Section 34.03.070).

Interest Required on Security Deposit: No. (Alaska Statutes, Section 34.03.070).

Separate Account required for Security Deposit: Yes. (Alaska Statutes, Section 34.03.070).

Additional Security Deposit Language in Lease: Yes, but required language is already in the leases in this book.

Exemption from Security Deposit Laws: Rental units that cost more than $2,000 per month are exempt. (Alaska Statutes, Section 34.03.070).

Notice Required to Change or Terminate Month-to-Month Tenancy: 30 days to terminate or change rent. (Alaska Statutes, Section 34.03.290(b)).

Number of Days for Pay Rent or Vacate Notice: 7 days.

Rent Late Fees: No statute.

Arizona

State Landlord-Tenant Statutes: Arizona Revised Statutes, Sections 33-1301 to 33-1381 and 12-1171 to -1183.

State Property Laws Statutes: Arizona Revised Statutes, Title 33.

State Law Website:
www.azleg.state.az.us/ArizonaRevisedStatutes.asp

State Real Estate Disclosure Laws: Affidavit of Disclosure. (This form is only required for the sale of real estate) (Arizona Revised Statutes, Section 33-422).

Landlord's Entry to Real Estate: Immediate access for emergency. 2 days notice for inspection, repairs, viewing of property and if tenant is absent for long periods. (Arizona Revised Statutes, Section 33-1343).

Security Deposit Amount Limits: 1 ½ month's rent. Landlord can charge more only if renter agrees. (Arizona Revised Statutes, Section 33-1321).

Deadlines for Security Deposit Returns: 14 days. (Arizona Revised Statutes, Section 33-1321).

Interest Required on Security Deposit: No. (Arizona Revised Statutes, Section 33-1321).

Separate Account required for Security Deposit: No. (Arizona Revised Statutes, Section 33-1321).

Additional Security Deposit Language in Lease: None.

Exemption from Security Deposit Laws: None. (Arizona Revised Statutes, Section 33-1321).

Notice Required to Change or Terminate Month-to-Month Tenancy: 30 days to terminate or change rent. (Arizona Revised Statutes, Section 33-1375).

Number of Days for Pay Rent or Vacate Notice: 5 days.

Rent Late Fees: Reasonable amount of late fee after nonpayment of rent for 5 days. (Arizona Revised Statutes, Section 33-1321).

Arkansas

State Landlord-Tenant Statutes: Arkansas Code, Sections 18-16-101 to 18-16-306.

State Property Laws Statutes: Arkansas Code, Title 18.

State Law Website:
www.arkleg.state.ar.us/NXT/gateway.dll?f=templates&fn=default.htm&vid=blr:code

State Real Estate Disclosure Laws: No statutory form.

Landlord's Entry to Real Estate: No Statute.

Security Deposit Amount Limits: 2 month's rent. (Arkansas Code, Section 18-16-303 to 18-16-306).

Deadlines for Security Deposit Returns: 30 days. (Arkansas Code, Section18-16-303 to 18-16-306).

Interest Required on Security Deposit: No. (Arkansas Code, Section 18-16-303 to 18-16-306).

Separate Account required for Security Deposit: No. (Arkansas Code, Section 18-16-303 to 18-16-306).

Additional Security Deposit Language in Lease: None.

Exemption from Security Deposit Laws: Does not apply to a landlord who owns 5 or less units. It does apply if the units are managed by another party for a fee. (Arkansas Code, Section 18-16-303 to 18-16-306).

Notice Required to Change or Terminate Month-to-Month Tenancy: 10 days to terminate or change rent. (Arkansas Code, Section 18-16-101).

Number of Days for Pay Rent or Vacate Notice: 10 days.

Rent Late Fees: No statute.

California

State Landlord-Tenant Statutes: California Civil Code, Sections 1940 to 1954.1 and 1954.50 to 1954.535 and 1961 to 1962.7.

State Property Laws Statutes: California Civil Code, Division 2, Part 2. Real or Immovable Property.

State Law Website: www.leginfo.ca.gov/calaw.html

State Real Estate Disclosure Laws: Smoke Detector Statement of Compliance, (CA Health and Safety Code 13113.8(b). Military Ordnance Disclosure (Civil Code 1102.15 and 1940.7). Industrial Use Disclosure, (Civil Code 1102.17). Earthquake Hazards Disclosure and Homeowner's Guide to Earthquake Safety, (CA Business and Professions Code 10149). Real Estate Transfer Disclosure Statement, (Civil Code Section 1102-1102.18). Natural Hazard Disclosure Statement, (Civil Code Section 1102-1102.18). (Certain of these forms are only necessary for the sale of real estate) Additional disclosures by a landlord may be required for the presence of mold, the presence of releases from controlled substances, disclosures relating to a tenant's gas or electric meter, and information relating to a database of registered sexual offenders (Health & Safety Code, Section 26147; Civil Code, Sections 1940.7.5, 1940.9, and 2079.10a) A California Addendum to Lease that provides the required notice regarding registered sexual offenders is provided on the Forms-on-CD. Landlords are advised however that they should check locally for information regarding required disclosures.

Landlord's Entry to Real Estate: Immediate access for emergency. 24 hour notice repairs and viewing of property. 48 hours for move out inspection. (California Civil Code, Section 1954).

Security Deposit Amount Limits: 2 months rent if unfurnished. 2 ½ month's rent if unfurnished and renter has a waterbed. 3 months rent if furnished. 3 ½ months rent if furnished with a waterbed. (California Civil Code, Sections 1950.5 and 1940.5(g)).

Deadlines for Security Deposit Returns: 3 weeks. (California Civil Code, Sections 1950.5 and 1940.5(g)).

Interest Required on Security Deposit: No. (California Civil Code, Sections 1950.5 and 1940.5(g)).

Separate Account required for Security Deposit: No. (California Civil Code, Sections 1950.5 and 1940.5(g)).

Additional Security Deposit Language in Lease: None.

Exemption from Security Deposit Laws: No. (California Civil Code, Sections 1950.5 and 1940.5(g)).

Notice Required to Change or Terminate Month-to-Month Tenancy: 30 days for tenant to terminate or change rent. 30 days for landlord to terminate or change rent. 60 days for landlord when raising rent or if tenancy is for over 1 year. (California Civil Code, Sections 1946, 827a, and 827b).

Number of Days for Pay Rent or Vacate Notice: 3 days.

Rent Late Fees: No statute. Late fees are unenforceable under California case law.

Colorado

State Landlord-Tenant Statutes: (Colorado Revised Statutes, Sections 38-12-101 to 38-12-104, 38-12-301 to 38-12-302).

State Property Laws Statutes: Colorado Revised Statutes, Title 38.

State Law Website: 198.187.128.12/

State Real Estate Disclosure Laws: Seller's Property Disclosure (Colorado Real Estate Commission SPD 19-10-05). (This form is only required for the sale of real estate).

Landlord's Entry to Real Estate: No Statute.

Security Deposit Amount Limits: No limit in statute. (Colorado Revised Statutes, Section 38-12-102 to 38-12-104).

Deadlines for Security Deposit Returns: 1 month unless rental agreement states otherwise, no more than 60 days. 72 hours if a hazardous situation concerning gas equipment requires renter to vacate property. (Colorado Revised Statutes, Section 38-12-102 to 38-12-104).

Interest Required on Security Deposit: No. (Colorado Revised Statutes, Section 38-12-102 to 38-12-104).

Separate Account required for Security Deposit: No. (Colorado Revised Statutes, Section 38-12-102 to 38-12-104).

Additional Security Deposit Language in Lease: None.

Exemption from Security Deposit Laws: None. (Colorado Revised Statutes, Section 38-12-102 to 38-12-104).

Notice Required to Change or Terminate Month-to-Month Tenancy: No statute.

Number of Days for Pay Rent or Vacate Notice: 3 days.

Rent Late Fees: No statute.

Connecticut

State Landlord-Tenant Statutes: Connecticut General Statutes, Sections 47a-1 to 47a-51.

State Property Laws Statutes: Connecticut General Statutes (see Volume 12, Section 47a).

State Law Website: www.cga.ct.gov/2005/pub/titles.htm

State Real Estate Disclosure Laws: Residential Property Condition Disclosure Report. (Connecticut General Statutes, Sections 20-327b). (This form is only required for the sale of real estate).

Landlord's Entry to Real Estate: Immediate access for emergency. Reasonable notice for inspection, repairs, viewing of property and if tenant is absent for long periods. (Connecticut General Statutes, Section 47a-16 to 47a-16a).

Security Deposit Amount Limits: 2 month's rent. 1 month's rent if renter is over the age of 62. (Connecticut General Statutes, Section 47a-21).

Deadlines for Security Deposit Returns: 30 days or within 15 days of receiving the renter's forwarding address. (Connecticut General Statutes, Section 47a-21).

Interest Required on Security Deposit: Yes. (Connecticut General Statutes, Section 47a-21).

Separate Account required for Security Deposit: Yes.. (Connecticut General Statutes, Section 47a-21).

Additional Security Deposit Language in Lease: None.

Exemption from Security Deposit Laws: None. (Connecticut General Statutes, Section 47a-21).

Notice Required to Change or Terminate Month-to-Month Tenancy: No statute.

Number of Days for Pay Rent or Vacate Notice: 3 days.

Rent Late Fees: 9 days after rent is due. (Connecticut General Statutes, Section 47a-15a).

Delaware

State Landlord-Tenant Statutes: Delaware Code, Title 25, Sections 5101-7013.

State Property Laws Statutes: Delaware Code, Title 25.

State Law Website: www.delcode.state.de.us/

State Real Estate Disclosure Laws: Seller's Disclosure of Real Property Condition Report. (Delaware Code, Title 6, Chapter 25, Subtitle VII, Buyer Property Protection Act. Sections, 2571-2578).(This form is only required for the sale of real estate).

Landlord's Entry to Real Estate: Immediate access for emergency. 2 days notice for inspection, repairs and viewing of property and if tenant is absent for long periods. (Delaware Code, Title 25, Sections, 5509 & 5510).

Security Deposit Amount Limits: 1 month's rent for rental agreements for one year or more. No limit on month-to-month rental agreements. Pet deposit can be up to an additional month's rent. (Delaware Code, Title 25, Section 5514).

Deadlines for Security Deposit Returns: 20 days. (Delaware Code, Title 25, Section 5514).

Interest Required on Security Deposit: No. (Delaware Code, Title 25, Section 5514).

Separate Account required for Security Deposit: Yes. (Delaware Code, Title 25, Section 5514).

Additional Security Deposit Language in Lease: None.

Exemption from Security Deposit Laws: None. (Delaware Code, Title 25, Section 5514).

Notice Required to Change or Terminate Month-to-Month Tenancy: 60 days to terminate or change rent. Renter had 15 days to terminate tenancy after changes. (Delaware Code, Title 25, Sections 5106 & 5107).

Number of Days for Pay Rent or Vacate Notice: 5 days.

Rent Late Fees: Cannot exceed 5% of rent after rent is more than 5 days late. (Delaware Code, Title 25, Section 5501(d)).

District of Columbia (Washington D.C.)

State Landlord-Tenant Statutes: District of Columbia Code Annotated, Sections 42-3201 to 42-4097 and 42-3501.01 to 42-3509.03.

State Property Laws Statutes: District of Columbia Code Annotated, Personal Property, Title 42 and Real Property, Title 45.

State Law Website: 198.187.128.12/

State Real Estate Disclosure Laws: No statutory form. (District of Columbia Code Annotated, Section 13-42-1301).

Landlord's Entry to Real Estate: No statute.

Security Deposit Amount Limits: 1 month's rent. (District of Columbia Code Annotated, Section 42.3502.17 and District of Columbia Municipal Regulations, Title 14, Sections, 308 to 311).

Deadlines for Security Deposit Returns: 45 days. (District of Columbia Code Annotated, Section 42.3502.17 and District of Columbia Municipal Regulations, Title 14, Sections, 308 to 311).

Interest Required on Security Deposit: Yes. (District of Columbia Code Annotated, Section 42.3502.17 and District of Columbia Municipal Regulations, Title 14, Sections, 308 to 311).

Separate Account required for Security Deposit: (District of Columbia Code Annotated, Section 42.3502.17 and District of Columbia Municipal Regulations, Title 14, Sections, 308 to 311).

Additional Security Deposit Language in Lease: None.

Exemption from Security Deposit Laws: None. (District of Columbia Code Annotated, Section 42.3502.17 and District of Columbia Municipal Regulations, Title 14, Sections, 308 to 311).

Notice Required to Change or Terminate Month-to-Month Tenancy: 30 days to terminate or change rent. (District of Columbia Code Annotated, Section 42-3202).

Number of Days for Pay Rent or Vacate Notice: 5 days.

Rent Late Fees: No statute.

Florida

State Landlord-Tenant Statutes: Florida Statutes, Sections 83.40-.66.

State Property Laws Statutes: Florida Statutes, Title XL., Ch.689-723.

State Law Website: www.flsenate.gov/Statutes/

State Real Estate Disclosure Laws: No statutory form. Landlords are required to provide tenant with fire and safety protection information. (Florida Statutes, Section 83.50).

Landlord's Entry to Real Estate: Immediate access for emergency. 12 hour notice for inspection, repairs and viewing of property and if tenant is absent for long periods. (Florida Statutes, Section 83.53).

Security Deposit Amount Limits: No limit in statute. (Florida Statutes, Section 83.53).

Deadlines for Security Deposit Returns: 15 to 60 days. This depends on if renter argues deductions. (Florida Statutes, Section 83.53).

Interest Required on Security Deposit: Are not required. (Florida Statutes, Section 83.53).

Separate Account required for Security Deposit: Yes. (Florida Statutes, Section 83.53).

Additional Security Deposit Language in Lease: .Yes. Must note the name and address of bank in which deposit is held.. If interest is to be paid, must indicate rate of interest on lease. Must also include this statement: "A copy of Florida Statutes regarding return of security deposits is attached to this lease." Also need to provided tenant with a copy of Florida Statutes, Section 83.49(3). Note: a copy of this statute is included on the Forms-on-CD. Additional note: you will need to use the text form of the residential leases in order to include the interest rate and security deposit notice on any leases that you use in Florida.

Exemption from Security Deposit Laws: None. (Florida Statutes, Section 83.53).

Notice Required to Change or Terminate Month-to-Month Tenancy: 15 days to terminate or change rent. (Florida Statutes, Section 83.57).

Number of Days for Pay Rent or Vacate Notice: 3 days.

Rent Late Fees: No statute.

Georgia

State Landlord-Tenant Statutes: Georgia Code, Sections 44-7-1 to 44-81.

State Property Laws Statutes: Georgia Code, Title 44.

State Law Website: www.legis.state.ga.us/legis/2005_06/05sumdocnet.htm

State Real Estate Disclosure Laws: No statutory form. Landlord must disclose if property has been flooded within the past 5 years. (Georgia Code, Section 44-7-20)

Landlord's Entry to Real Estate: No statute.

Security Deposit Amount Limits: No limit in statute. (Georgia Code, Sections 44-7-30 to 44-7-37).

Deadlines for Security Deposit Returns: 1 month. (Georgia Code, Sections 44-7-30 to 44-7-37).

Interest Required on Security Deposit: No. (Georgia Code, Sections 44-7-30 to 44-7-37).

Separate Account required for Security Deposit: Yes. (Georgia Code, Sections 44-7-30 to 44-7-37).

Additional Security Deposit Language in Lease: Yes. Must indicate on lease the name, address, and account number where deposits are held..

Exemption from Security Deposit Laws: Exemption for landlord who owns 10 or less rental units. Exemption does not apply if rental units are managed by an outside agency. (Georgia Code, Sections 44-7-30 to 44-7-37).

Notice Required to Change or Terminate Month-to-Month Tenancy: 30 days for tenant to terminate or change rent. 60 days for landlord to terminate or change rent. (Georgia Code, Sections 44-7-7).

Number of Days for Pay Rent or Vacate Notice: 7 days.
Rent Late Fees: No statute.

Hawaii

State Landlord-Tenant Statutes: Hawaii Revised Statutes, Sections 521-1 to 521-78.
State Property Laws Statutes: Hawaii Revised Statutes, Volume 12, Chapter 0501 to 0588.
State Law Website: www.capitol.hawaii.gov/hrscurrent/?press1=docs
State Real Estate Disclosure Laws: No statutory form. (Hawaii Revised Statutes 508D-4(2)). Landlord must provide tenant with landlord's state excise tax number to allow tenant to apply for low-income tax credit. (Hawaii Revised Statutes, Section 521-43).
Landlord's Entry to Real Estate: Immediate access for emergency. 2 day notice for inspection, repairs and viewing of property and if tenant is absent for long periods. (Hawaii Revised Statutes, Sections 521-53 to 521-70(b)).
Security Deposit Amount Limits: 1 month's rent. (Hawaii Revised Statutes, Section 521-44).
Deadlines for Security Deposit Returns: 14 days. (Hawaii Revised Statutes, Section 521-44).
Interest Required on Security Deposit: No. (Hawaii Revised Statutes, Section 521-44).
Separate Account required for Security Deposit: No. (Hawaii Revised Statutes, Section 521-44).
Additional Security Deposit Language in Lease: None.
Exemption from Security Deposit Laws: None. (Hawaii Revised Statutes, Section 521-44).
Notice Required to Change or Terminate Month-to-Month Tenancy: 28 days for tenant to terminate or change rent. 45 days for landlord to terminate or change rent. (Hawaii Revised Statutes, Section 521-71, 521-21(d)).
Number of Days for Pay Rent or Vacate Notice: 5 days.
Rent Late Fees: No statute.

Idaho

State Landlord-Tenant Statutes: Idaho Code, Sections 55-201 to 55-313 and 6-301 to 6-324.
State Property Laws Statutes: Idaho Code, Title 55.
State Law Website: www3.state.id.us/idstat/TOC/idstTOC.html
State Real Estate Disclosure Laws: Seller Property Disclosure Form. (Idaho Code, Section 55-2501). (This form is only required for the sale of real estate).
Landlord's Entry to Real Estate: No statute.
Security Deposit Amount Limits: No limit in statute. (Idaho Code, Section 6-321).
Deadlines for Security Deposit Returns: 21 days. Up to 30 days if both parties agree. (Idaho Code, Section 6-321).
Interest Required on Security Deposit: No. (Idaho Code, Section 6-321).
Separate Account required for Security Deposit: No. (Idaho Code, Section 6-321).
Additional Security Deposit Language in Lease: None.
Exemption from Security Deposit Laws: None. (Idaho Code, Section 6-321).
Notice Required to Change or Terminate Month-to-Month Tenancy: 1 month notice for tenant to terminate or change rent. 1 month notice for landlord to terminate rent. Landlord must provide 15 day's notice to increase rent or change tenancy. (Idaho Code, Sections 55-208 and 55-307).
Number of Days for Pay Rent or Vacate Notice: 3 days.
Rent Late Fees: No statute.

Illinois

State Landlord-Tenant Statutes: Illinois Compiled Statutes, Chapter. 765, Sections 705/0.01 to 740/5.

State Property Laws Statutes: Illinois Compiled Statutes, Chapter 765.

State Law Website: www.ilga.gov/legislation/ilcs/ilcs.asp

State Real Estate Disclosure Laws: Residential Real Property Disclosure Report. (Illinois Compiled Statutes, Chapter. 765 ILCS 77). (This form is only required for the sale of real estate). Landlord may need to provide disclosure to tenant regarding electric or gas meters for rented property if such meters serve areas outside of rented property. (Illinois Complied Statutes, 735 ILCS 1.2 and 740 ILCS 5). In addition there are additional forms required for leases within the City of Chicago: Chicago Addendum to Lease; Chicago Heating Disclosure Form: Chicago Residential Landlord and Tenant Ordinance Summary. The Chicago forms are provided on the Forms-on-CD.

Landlord's Entry to Real Estate: No statute.

Security Deposit Amount Limits: No limit in statute. (Illinois Compiled Statutes, Chapter. 765, Sections 710/0.01 to 715/3).

Deadlines for Security Deposit Returns: 30 days. Up to 45 days if renter argues deductions. (Illinois Compiled Statutes, Chapter. 765, Sections 710/0.01 to 715/3).

Interest Required on Security Deposit: Required for landlords with more than 25 rental units. (Illinois Compiled Statutes, Chapter. 765, Sections 710/0.01 to 715/3).

Separate Account required for Security Deposit: No. (Illinois Compiled Statutes, Chapter. 765, Sections 710/0.01 to 715/3).

Additional Security Deposit Language in Lease: None.

Exemption from Security Deposit Laws: Landlords with 4 or less rental units are exempt. (Illinois Compiled Statutes, Chapter. 765, Sections 710/0.01 to 715/3).

Notice Required to Change or Terminate Month-to-Month Tenancy: 30 days to terminate or change rent. (Illinois Compiled Statutes, Chapter. 735, Section 5/9-207).

Number of Days for Pay Rent or Vacate Notice: 5 days.

Rent Late Fees: No statute.

Indiana

State Landlord-Tenant Statutes: Indiana Code, Sections 32-31-1-1 to 32-31-8-6.

State Property Laws Statutes: Indiana Code, Title 32.

State Law Website: www.in.gov/legislative/ic/code/

State Real Estate Disclosure Laws: Seller's Residential Real Estate Sales Disclosure. (Indiana Code, Section 24-4.6-2). (This form is only required for the sale of real estate).

Landlord's Entry to Real Estate: No statute.

Security Deposit Amount Limits: No limits in statute. (Indiana Code, Sections 32-31-3-9 to 32-31-3-19).

Deadlines for Security Deposit Returns: 45 days. (Indiana Code, Sections 32-31-3-9 to 32-31-3-19).

Interest Required on Security Deposit: No. (Indiana Code, Sections 32-31-3-9 to 32-31-3-19).

Separate Account required for Security Deposit: No. (Indiana Code, Sections 32-31-3-9 to 32-31-3-19).

Additional Security Deposit Language in Lease: None.

Exemption from Security Deposit Laws: None. (Indiana Code, Sections 32-31-3-9 to 32-31-3-19).

Notice Required to Change or Terminate Month-to-Month Tenancy: 1 month to terminate or change rent. (Indiana Code, Sections 32-31-1-1).

Number of Days for Pay Rent or Vacate Notice: 10 days.

Rent Late Fees: No statute.

Iowa

State Landlord-Tenant Statutes: Iowa Code Annotated, Sections 562A.1-.36.

State Property Laws Statutes: Iowa Code, Title XIV.

State Law Website: www.legis.state.ia.us/ IACODE/1999/titles.html

State Real Estate Disclosure Laws: Residential Property Seller Disclosure Statement. (Iowa Code Annotated, Section 558A.1). (This form is only required for the sale of real estate). Landlords are required to provide tenants with a full explanation of all utility rates, charges, and services. (Iowa Code Annotated, Section 562a.13(4).

Landlord's Entry to Real Estate: Immediate access for emergency. 24 hour notice for inspection, repairs, viewing of property and if tenant is absent for long periods. (Iowa Code Annotated, Sections 562A.19, 562A.28 and 562A.29).

Security Deposit Amount Limits: 2 month's rent. (Iowa Code Annotated, Section 562A.12).

Deadlines for Security Deposit Returns: 30 days. (Iowa Code Annotated, Section 562A.12).

Interest Required on Security Deposit: Interest payments are not required. (Iowa Code Annotated, Section 562A.12).

Separate Account required for Security Deposit: Yes. (Iowa Code Annotated, Section 562A.12).

Additional Security Deposit Language in Lease: None.

Exemption from Security Deposit Laws: None. (Iowa Code Annotated, Section 562A.12).

Notice Required to Change or Terminate Month-to-Month Tenancy: 30 days to terminate or change rent. (Iowa Code Annotated, Sections 562A.34 and 562A.13(5)).

Number of Days for Pay Rent or Vacate Notice: 3 days.

Rent Late Fees: Late fees cannot exceed $10.00 per day or $40.00 a month. (Iowa Code Annotated, Section 535.2(7)).

Kansas

State Landlord-Tenant Statutes: Kansas Statutes, Sections 58-2501 to 58-2573.

State Property Laws Statutes: Kansas Statutes, Chapters 58 and 67.

State Law Website: www.kslegislature.org/legsrv-statutes/ index.do?bill=58-2501

State Real Estate Disclosure Laws: No statutory form.

Landlord's Entry to Real Estate: Immediate access for emergency. "Reasonable" notice for inspection, repairs, viewing of property and if tenant is absent for long periods. (Kansas Statutes, Sections 58-2557 and 58-2565).

Security Deposit Amount Limits: 1 month's rent unfurnished. 1 ½ month's rent furnished. Additional ½ month's rent for pet deposit. (Kansas Statutes, Section 58-2550).

Deadlines for Security Deposit Returns: 30 days. (Kansas Statutes, Section 58-2550).

Interest Required on Security Deposit: No. (Kansas Statutes, Section 58-2550).

Separate Account required for Security Deposit: No. (Kansas Statutes, Section 58-2550).

Additional Security Deposit Language in Lease: None.

Exemption from Security Deposit Laws: None. (Kansas Statutes, Section 58-2550).

Notice Required to Change or Terminate Month-to-Month Tenancy: 30 days to terminate rent. No amount of notice in statute for changing rent. (Kansas Statutes, Section 58-2550).

Number of Days for Pay Rent or Vacate Notice: 3 days.(if the pay period for the lease is 3 months or less). 10 days if the lease pay period is over 3 months.

Rent Late Fees: No statute.

Kentucky

State Landlord-Tenant Statutes: Kentucky Revised Statutes, Sections 383.010 to 383.715.

State Property Laws Statutes: Kentucky Revised Statutes, Title XXXII.

State Law Website: www.lrc.state.ky.us/KRS/383-00/CHAPTER.HTM.

State Real Estate Disclosure Laws: Seller's Disclosure of Property Conditions. (Kentucky Revised Statutes, Section 324.360). (This form is only required for the sale of real estate).

Landlord's Entry to Real Estate: Immediate access for emergency. 2 day notice for inspection, repairs and viewing of property and if tenant is absent for long periods. (Kentucky Revised Statutes, Section 383.615).

Security Deposit Amount Limits: No limit in statute. (Kentucky Revised Statutes, Section 383.580).

Deadlines for Security Deposit Returns: 30 days. Up to 60 days if renter argues deductions. (Kentucky Revised Statutes, Section 383.580).

Interest Required on Security Deposit: No. (Kentucky Revised Statutes, Section 383.580).

Separate Account required for Security Deposit: Yes. (Kentucky Revised Statutes, Section 383.580).

Additional Security Deposit Language in Lease: Yes. Must indicate on lease the name, address, and account number where deposits are held.

Exemption from Security Deposit Laws: None. (Kentucky Revised Statutes, Section 383.580).

Notice Required to Change or Terminate Month-to-Month Tenancy: 30 days to terminate or change rent. (Kentucky Revised Statutes, Section 383.695).

Number of Days for Pay Rent or Vacate Notice: 7 days.

Rent Late Fees: No statute.

Louisiana

State Landlord-Tenant Statutes: Louisiana Revised Statutes Annotated, Sections 9:3201 to 9:3259 and Louisiana Civil Code Annotated Article 2669 to 2742.

State Property Laws Statutes: Louisiana Revised Statutes Annotated, Title 9, Civil Code Ancillaries, Louisiana Civil Code, Louisiana Code of Civil procedure.

State Law Website: www.legis.state.la.us/

State Real Estate Disclosure Laws: Property Disclosure Document for Residential Real Estate. (Louisiana Revised Statutes Annotated, Title 9, Civil Code Ancillaries, Section 9: 3198). (This form is only required for the sale of real estate).

Landlord's Entry to Real Estate: No statute.

Security Deposit Amount Limits: No limit in statute. (Louisiana Revised Statutes Annotated, Sections 9:3251 to 9:3254).

Deadlines for Security Deposit Returns: 1 month. (Louisiana Revised Statutes Annotated, Sections 9:3251 to 9:3254).

Interest Required on Security Deposit: No. (Louisiana Revised Statutes Annotated, Sections 9:3251 to 9:3254).

Separate Account required for Security Deposit: No. (Louisiana Revised Statutes Annotated, Sections 9:3251 to 9:3254).

Additional Security Deposit Language in Lease: None.

Exemption from Security Deposit Laws: None. (Louisiana Revised Statutes Annotated, Sections 9:3251 to 9:3254).

Notice Required to Change or Terminate Month-to-Month Tenancy: 10 days to terminate or change rent. (Louisiana Civil Code Annotated, Article 2686).

Number of Days for Pay Rent or Vacate Notice: 10 days. Must be 10 days notice prior to the end of the current month.

Rent Late Fees: No statute.

Maine

State Landlord-Tenant Statutes: Maine Revised Statutes, Title 14, Sections 6021 to 6046.

State Property Laws Statutes: Maine Revised Statutes Title 33.

State Law Website: janus.state.me.us/legis/statutes/

State Real Estate Disclosure Laws: Property Disclosure Statement. (Maine Revised Statutes, Section 33-7-1A-171) (This form is only required for the sale of real estate).

Landlord's Entry to Real Estate: Immediate access for emergency. 24 hour notice for inspection, repairs and viewing of property and if tenant is absent for long periods. (Maine Revised Statutes, Title 14, Section 6024).

Security Deposit Amount Limits: 2 month's rent. (Maine Revised Statutes, Title 14, Sections 6031 to 6038).

Deadlines for Security Deposit Returns: 30 days if rental agreement is in writing. 21 days if agreement is verbal. (Maine Revised Statutes, Title 14, Sections 6031 to 6038).

Interest Required on Security Deposit: No. (Maine Revised Statutes, Title 14, Sections 6031 to 6038).

Separate Account required for Security Deposit: Yes. (Maine Revised Statutes, Title 14, Sections 6031 to 6038).

Additional Security Deposit Language in Lease: None.

Exemption from Security Deposit Laws: Exemption if rental structure has 5 or less rental units and the landlord is also living in one of the rental units. (Maine Revised Statutes, Title 14, Sections 6031 to 6038).

Notice Required to Change or Terminate Month-to-Month Tenancy: 30 days to terminate rent. Landlord must provide 45 day's notice to increase rent. (Maine Revised Statutes, Title 14, Sections 6002 and 6015).

Number of Days for Pay Rent or Vacate Notice: 7 days.

Rent Late Fees: Late fees cannot exceed 4% of the amount due for 30 days. Landlord must notify in writing any late fee at the start of tenancy and cannot impose it until rent is 15 days late. (Maine Revised Statutes, Title 14, Section 6028).

Maryland

State Landlord-Tenant Statutes: Maryland Code, Real Property, Sections 8-101 to 8-604.

State Property Laws Statutes: Maryland Code, Real Property.

State Law Website: 198.187.128.12/

State Real Estate Disclosure Laws: Residential Property Disclosure and Disclaimer Statement. (Maryland Code, Real Property, Section 10-702). (This form is only required for the sale of real estate).

Landlord's Entry to Real Estate: No statute.

Security Deposit Amount Limits: 2 month's rent. (Maryland Code, Real Property, Sections 8-203 to 8-203.1).

Deadlines for Security Deposit Returns: 30 days. Up to 45 days if renter was evicted or abandoned the rental unit. (Maryland Code, Real Property, Sections 8-203 to 8-203.1).

Interest Required on Security Deposit: Yes. (Maryland Code, Real Property, Sections 8-203 to 8-203.1).

Separate Account required for Security Deposit: Yes. (Maryland Code, Real Property, Sections 8-203 to 8-203.1).

Additional Security Deposit Language in Lease: Yes. The following language must be included in the lease: "If tenant requests, a written list of existing damages will be supplied to the tenant by USPS Certified mail within 15 days of occupancy." Note: the text version of the leases must be used to include this language in leases in Maryland.

Exemption from Security Deposit Laws: None. (Maryland Code, Real Property, Sections 8-203 to 8-203.1).

Notice Required to Change or Terminate Month-to-Month Tenancy: 1 month to terminate or change rent. 2 month's notice in Montgomery County. Does not apply to Baltimore. (Maryland Code, Real Property, Sections 8-402(b)(3) and 8-402(b)(4)).

Number of Days for Pay Rent or Vacate Notice: 9 days. This period provides for 5 days to appear in court and then an additional 4 days to vacate the property.

Rent Late Fees: Late fees cannot exceed 5% of the rent due. (Maryland Code, Real Property, Sections 8-208(d)(3)).

Massachusetts

State Landlord-Tenant Statutes: Massachusetts General Laws, Chapter 186, Section 1-21.

State Property Laws Statutes: Massachusetts General Laws, Part I, Real And Personal Property And Domestic Relations, Chapters 183-189.

State Law Website: www.mass.gov/legis/laws/mgl/index.htm

State Real Estate Disclosure Laws: No statutory form.

Landlord's Entry to Real Estate: Immediate access for emergencies; may enter for inspections for damages during last 30 days of lease; may enter if property appears abandoned. Lease may provide landlord access for repairs, reasonable inspections, and to show the premises to a prospective tenant or buyer. (Massachusetts General Laws, Chapter 186, Section 15B(1)(a)).

Security Deposit Amount Limits: 1 month's rent. (Massachusetts General Laws, Chapter 186, Section 15B).

Deadlines for Security Deposit Returns: 30 days. (Massachusetts General Laws, Chapter 186, Section 15B).

Interest Required on Security Deposit: Yes. (Massachusetts General Laws, Chapter 186, Section 15B).

Separate Account required for Security Deposit: Yes. (Massachusetts General Laws, Chapter 186, Section 15B).

Additional Security Deposit Language in Lease: None.

Exemption from Security Deposit Laws: None. (Massachusetts General Laws, Chapter 186, Section 15B).

Notice Required to Change or Terminate Month-to-Month Tenancy: Length of tenancy period or 30 days (whichever is longer). (Massachusetts General Laws, Chapter 186, Section 12).

Number of Days for Pay Rent or Vacate Notice: 14 days.

Rent Late Fees: Late fees, including interest on late rent, cannot be imposed until the rent is 30 days late. (Massachusetts General Laws, Chapter 186, Section 15B(1)(c)).

Michigan

State Landlord-Tenant Statutes: Michigan Compiled Laws, Section 554.601-.640.

State Property Laws Statutes: Michigan Compiled Laws, Chapters 554 to 570.

State Law Website: www.legislature.mi.gov/

State Real Estate Disclosure Laws: Seller's Disclosure Statement. (Michigan Compiled Laws, Section 565.957). (This form is only required for the sale of real estate).

Landlord's Entry to Real Estate: No statute.

Security Deposit Amount Limits: 1 ½ month's rent. (Michigan Compiled Laws, Sections 554.602 to 554.613).

Deadlines for Security Deposit Returns: 30 days. (Michigan Compiled Laws, Sections 554.602 to 554.613).

Interest Required on Security Deposit: No. (Michigan Compiled Laws, Sections 554.602 to 554.613).

Separate Account required for Security Deposit: Yes. (Michigan Compiled Laws, Sections 554.602 to 554.613).

Additional Security Deposit Language in Lease: Yes. The name and address of the bank which holds the security deposits must be noted on the lease. In addition, the following language must be included in the lease in at least 12 point type: "The tenant must notify the landlord in writing, within 4 days after moving out, of a forwarding address where tenant can be reached and receive mail. If tenant does not supply a forwarding address the landlord will not be required to send tenant an itemized list of damages." Note: the text versions of the leases must be used in order to prepare leases in Michigan.

Exemption from Security Deposit Laws: None. (Michigan Compiled Laws, Sections 554.602 to 554.613).

Notice Required to Change or Terminate Month-to-Month Tenancy: Length of tenancy period. (Michigan Compiled Laws, Sections 554.134).

Number of Days for Pay Rent or Vacate Notice: 7 days.

Rent Late Fees: No statute.

Minnesota

State Landlord-Tenant Statutes: Minnesota Statutes Sections 504B.001 to 504B.471.

State Property Laws Statutes: Minnesota Statutes, Chapters 554-570.

State Law Website: www.revisor.leg.state. mn.us/stats/

State Real Estate Disclosure Laws: Minnesota law requires disclosure of any wells on property being sold. (Minnesota Statutes, Section 103I.235) In addition, landlords are required to provide tenants with various disclosures relating to property inspection orders, condemnation orders, unfit for habitation declarations, and any citations for health, safety, zoning, or other code violations. (Minnesota Statutes, Section 504B.195).

Landlord's Entry to Real Estate: Immediate access for emergency. "Reasonable" notice for inspection, repairs and viewing of property. (Minnesota Statutes, Section 504B.211).

Security Deposit Amount Limits: No limit in statute. (Minnesota Statutes, Sections 504B.175 to 504B.178).

Deadlines for Security Deposit Returns: 3 weeks. 5 days if rental unit is condemned. (Minnesota Statutes, Sections 504B.175 to 504B.178).

Interest Required on Security Deposit: Yes. (Minnesota Statutes, Sections 504B.175 to 504B.178).

Separate Account required for Security Deposit: No. (Minnesota Statutes, Sections 504B.175 to 504B.178).

Additional Security Deposit Language in Lease: None.

Exemption from Security Deposit Laws: None. (Minnesota Statutes, Sections 504B.175 to 504B.178).

Notice Required to Change or Terminate Month-to-Month Tenancy: Length between time rent is due. (Minnesota Statutes, Section 504B.135).

Number of Days for Pay Rent or Vacate Notice: 14 days.

Rent Late Fees: No statute.

Mississippi

State Landlord-Tenant Statutes: Mississippi Code, Sections 89-8-1 to 89-8-27.

State Property Laws Statutes: Mississippi Code, Title 89.

State Law Website: 198.187.128.12

State Real Estate Disclosure Laws: Seller's Disclosure Statement. (Mississippi Code, Section 89-1-501). (This form is only required for the sale of real estate).

Landlord's Entry to Real Estate: No statute.

Security Deposit Amount Limits: No limit in statute. (Mississippi Code, Section 89-8-21).

Deadlines for Security Deposit Returns: 45 days. (Mississippi Code, Section 89-8-21).

Interest Required on Security Deposit: No. (Mississippi Code, Section 89-8-21).

Separate Account required for Security Deposit: No. (Mississippi Code, Section 89-8-21).

Additional Security Deposit Language in Lease: Exemption from Security Deposit Laws: None. (Mississippi Code, Section 89-8-21).

Notice Required to Change or Terminate Month-to-Month Tenancy: 30 days to terminate or change rent. (Mississippi Code, Section 89-8-19).

Number of Days for Pay Rent or Vacate Notice: 3 days.

Rent Late Fees: No statute.

Missouri

State Landlord-Tenant Statutes: Missouri Revised Statutes, Sections 441.005 to 441.880 and 535.150 to 535.300.

State Property Laws Statutes: Missouri Revised Statutes, Title 29.

State Law Website: ww.moga.state.mo.us/STATUTES/STATUTES.HTM

State Real Estate Disclosure Laws: No statutory form.

Landlord's Entry to Real Estate: No statute.

Security Deposit Amount Limits: 2 month's rent. (Missouri Revised Statutes, Section 535.300).

Deadlines for Security Deposit Returns: 30 days. (Missouri Revised Statutes, Section 535.300).

Interest Required on Security Deposit: No. (Missouri Revised Statutes, Section 535.300).

Separate Account required for Security Deposit: No. (Missouri Revised Statutes, Section 535.300).

Additional Security Deposit Language in Lease: None.

Exemption from Security Deposit Laws: None. (Missouri Revised Statutes, Section 535.300).

Notice Required to Change or Terminate Month-to-Month Tenancy: 1 month to terminate or change rent. (Missouri Revised Statutes, Section 441.060).

Number of Days for Pay Rent or Vacate Notice: Immediately.

Rent Late Fees: No statute.

Montana

State Landlord-Tenant Statutes: Montana Code, Sections 70-24-101 to 70-25-206.

State Property Laws Statutes: Montana Code, Title 70.

State Law Website: data.opi.state.mt.us/bills/mca_toc/index.htm

State Real Estate Disclosure Laws: No statutory form.

Landlord's Entry to Real Estate: Immediate access for emergency. 24 hour notice for inspection, repairs and viewing of property and if tenant is absent for long periods. (Montana Code, Section 70-24-312).

Security Deposit Amount Limits: No limit in statute. (Montana Code, Sections 70-25-101 to 70-25-206).

Deadlines for Security Deposit Returns: 30 days. 10 days if no deductions are made. (Montana Code Sections 70-25-101 to 70-25-206).

Interest Required on Security Deposit: No. (Montana Code Sections 70-25-101 to 70-25-206).

Separate Account required for Security Deposit: No. (Montana Code Sections 70-25-101 to 70-25-206).

Additional Security Deposit Language in Lease: None.

Exemption from Security Deposit Laws: None. (Montana Code Sections 70-25-101 to 70-25-206).

Notice Required to Change or Terminate Month-to-Month Tenancy: 30 days to terminate or change rent. (Montana Code, Section 70-24-441).

Number of Days for Pay Rent or Vacate Notice: 3 days.

Rent Late Fees: No statute.

Nebraska

State Landlord-Tenant Statutes: Nebraska Statutes, Sections 76-1401 to 76-1449.

State Property Laws Statutes: Nebraska Statutes, Chapters 69 and 76.

State Law Website: srvwww.unicam.state.ne.us/Laws2005.html

State Real Estate Disclosure Laws: Seller Property Condition Disclosure Statement. (Nebraska Statutes, Section 76-2-120). (This form is only required for the sale of real estate).

Landlord's Entry to Real Estate: Immediate access for emergency. 1 day notice for inspection, repairs and viewing of property and if tenant is absent for long periods. (Nebraska Statutes, Section 76-1423).

Security Deposit Amount Limits: No limit in statute. (Nebraska Statutes, Section 76-1416).

Deadlines for Security Deposit Returns: 14 days. (Nebraska Statutes, Section 76-1416).

Interest Required on Security Deposit: No. (Nebraska Statutes, Section 76-1416).

Separate Account required for Security Deposit: No. (Nebraska Statutes, Section 76-1416).

Additional Security Deposit Language in Lease: None.

Exemption from Security Deposit Laws: None. (Nebraska Statutes, Section 76-1416).

Notice Required to Change or Terminate Month-to-Month Tenancy: 30 days to terminate or change rent. (Nebraska Statutes, Section 76-1437).

Number of Days for Pay Rent or Vacate Notice: 3 days.

Rent Late Fees: No statute.

Nevada

State Landlord-Tenant Statutes: Nevada Revised Statute Annotated, Sections 118A.010 - 118A.520.

State Property Laws Statutes: Nevada Revised Statute Annotated, Title 10.

State Law Website: www.leg.state.nv.us/NRS/

State Real Estate Disclosure Laws: Seller's Real Property Disclosure Form. (Nevada Revised Statute Annotated, Section 133.060). (This form is only required for the sale of real estate).

Landlord's Entry to Real Estate: Immediate access for emergency. 24 hour notice for inspection, repairs and viewing of property and if tenant is absent for long periods. (Nevada Revised Statute Annotated, Section 118A.330).

Security Deposit Amount Limits: 3 month's rent. (Nevada Revised Statute Annotated, Sections 118A.240 to 118A.250).

Deadlines for Security Deposit Returns: 30 days. (Nevada Revised Statute Annotated, Sections 118A.240 to 118A.250).

Interest Required on Security Deposit: No. (Nevada Revised Statute Annotated, Sections 118A.240 to 118A.250).

Separate Account required for Security Deposit: No. (Nevada Revised Statute Annotated, Sections 118A.240 to 118A.250).

Additional Security Deposit Language in Lease: None.

Exemption from Security Deposit Laws: None. (Nevada Revised Statute Annotated, Sections 118A.240 to 118A.250).

Notice Required to Change or Terminate Month-to-Month Tenancy: 30 days to terminate. Landlord must give 45 day notice to raise rent. (Nevada Revised Statute Annotated, Sections 40.251 and 118A.300).

Number of Days for Pay Rent or Vacate Notice: 5 days.

Rent Late Fees: Must be in writing. (Nevada Revised Statute Annotated, Sections 118A.200(2)(g) and 118A.200(3)(c)).

New Hampshire

State Landlord-Tenant Statutes: New Hampshire Revised Statutes, Sections 540:1 to 540:29 and 540-A:1 to 540-A:8.

State Property Laws Statutes: New Hampshire Revised Statutes, Titles 46 to 48.

State Law Website: www.gencourt.state.nh.us/rsa/html/indexes/540.html

State Real Estate Disclosure Laws: No statutory form.

Landlord's Entry to Real Estate: Immediate access for emergency. "Reasonable" notice and prior consent are required for inspection, repairs, viewing of property and entry if tenant is absent for long periods. (New Hampshire Revised Statutes, Section 540-A:3).

Security Deposit Amount Limits: 1 month's rent or $100.00 (which ever is greater). No limit but in writing, if owner resides on the premises. (New Hampshire Revised Statutes, Sections 540-A:5 to 540-A:8 and 540-B: 10).

Deadlines for Security Deposit Returns: 30 days. If it is a shared facility and if it is more than 1 month's rent, an agreement must be written stating how much the deposit is and when it will be returned. If no written agreement, deposit must be returned within 20 days. (New Hampshire Revised Statutes, Sections 540-A:5 to 540-A:8 and 540-B:10).

Interest Required on Security Deposit: Yes. (New Hampshire Revised Statutes, Sections 540-A:5 to 540-A:8 and 540-B:10).

Separate Account required for Security Deposit: Yes. (New Hampshire Revised Statutes, Sections 540-A:5 to 540-A:8 and 540-B:10).

Additional Security Deposit Language in Lease: None.

Exemption from Security Deposit Laws: Exemption for a person who rents or leases a single family residence and owns no other rental property or who rents or leases rental units in an owner-occupied building of 5 units or less shall not be considered a "landlord"

for the purposes of this subdivision, except for any individual unit in such building which is occupied by a person or persons 60 years of age or older. Exemption also applies for vacation property. (New Hampshire Revised Statutes, Section 540-A:8).

Notice Required to Change or Terminate Month-to-Month Tenancy: 30 days to terminate or change rent. Landlord must have "just cause" for termination. (New Hampshire Revised Statutes, Section 540:2 and 540:3).

Number of Days for Pay Rent or Vacate Notice: 7 days for a lease and 30 days for a month-to-month rental agreement.

Rent Late Fees: No statute.

New Jersey

State Landlord-Tenant Statutes: New Jersey Statutes Annotated, Sections 2A:18-61.40 to 2A:18-61.52.

State Property Laws Statutes: New Jersey Statutes Annotated, Title 46.

State Law Website: lis.njleg.state.nj.us/

State Real Estate Disclosure Laws: No statutory form.

Landlord's Entry to Real Estate: No statute.

Security Deposit Amount Limits: 1 ½ month's rent. (New Jersey Statutes Annotated, Sections 46:8-19 to 46:8-26).

Deadlines for Security Deposit Returns: 30 days. Return deposit in 5 days in case of fire, flood, condemnation or evacuation. (New Jersey Statutes Annotated, Sections 46:8-19 to 46:8-26).

Interest Required on Security Deposit: Yes. (New Jersey Statutes Annotated, Sections 46:8-19 to 46:8-26).

Separate Account required for Security Deposit: Yes. (New Jersey Statutes Annotated, Sections 46:8-19 to 46:8-26).

Additional Security Deposit Language in Lease: None.

Exemption from Security Deposit Laws: Rental units in owner-occupied buildings that have no more than two units other than the owner-landlord's unit unless tenants in have sent a 30-day written notice to the landlord stating that he or she wants the landlord to comply with the law's provisions. (New Jersey Statutes Annotated, Section 46:8-19 to 46:8-26).

Notice Required to Change or Terminate Month-to-Month Tenancy: No statute.

Number of Days for Pay Rent or Vacate Notice: 30 days. Landlord must accept rent due any time up to the date of trial.

Rent Late Fees: Landlord must wait until 5 days to charge late fee. (New Jersey Statutes Annotated, Section 2A:42-6.1).

New Mexico

State Landlord-Tenant Statutes: New Mexico Statutes Annotated, Sections 47-8-1 to 47-8-51 (rev. 01/06).

State Property Laws Statutes: New Mexico Statutes Annotated, Chapter 42.

State Law Website: www.conwaygreene.com/NewMexico.htm

State Real Estate Disclosure Laws: No statutory form.

Landlord's Entry to Real Estate: Immediate access for emergency. 24 hour notice for inspection, repairs, viewing and entry if tenant is absent for long periods. (New Mexico Statutes Annotated, Section 47-8-24).

Security Deposit Amount Limits: 1 month's rent for rental agreements less than a year. No limit for leases over one year. (New Mexico Statutes Annotated, Section 47-8-18).

Deadlines for Security Deposit Returns: 30 days. (New Mexico Statutes Annotated, Section 47-8-18).

Interest Required on Security Deposit: Yes. (New Mexico Statutes Annotated, Section 47-8-18).

Separate Account required for Security Deposit: No. (New Mexico Statutes Annotated, Section 47-8-18).

Additional Security Deposit Language in Lease: None.

Exemption from Security Deposit Laws: None. (New Mexico Statutes Annotated, Section 47-8-18).

Notice Required to Change or Terminate Month-to-Month Tenancy: 30 days to terminate or change rent. (New Mexico Statutes Annotated, Section 47-8-37 and 47-8-15(F)).

Number of Days for Pay Rent or Vacate Notice: 3 days.

Rent Late Fees: Late fee cannot exceed 10% of the rent. (New Mexico Statutes Annotated, Section 47-8-15(D)).

New York

State Landlord-Tenant Statutes: New York Consolidated Laws Real Property Law (RPL) Sections 220-238; Real Property Actions and Proceedings Law (RPAPL) Sections 701-853; Multiple Dwelling Law (MDL) all; Multiple Residence Law (MRL) all; General Obligation Law (GOL) Sections 7-103-108.

State Property Laws Statutes: New York Consolidated Laws, Real Property Chapter 50.

State Law Website: public.leginfo.state.ny.us/menugetf.cgi

State Real Estate Disclosure Laws: Property Condition Disclosure Statement. (New York Consolidated Laws, Real Property (RP) 14-460). (This form is only required for the sale of real estate).

Landlord's Entry to Real Estate: No statute. A landlord, however, may enter a tenant's apartment with reasonable prior notice, and at a reasonable time: (a) to provide necessary or agreed upon repairs or services; or (b) in accordance with the lease; or (c) to show the apartment to prospective purchasers or tenants. In emergencies, such as fires, the landlord may enter the apartment without the tenant's consent. (Tenant's Rights Guide, New York State Attorney General Office).

Security Deposit Amount Limits: No limit in statutes for non-regulated units. (New York Consolidated General Obligation Law (GOL), Sections 7-103 to 7-108).

Deadlines for Security Deposit Returns: Within a reasonable amount of time. (New York Consolidated General Obligation Law (GOL), Sections 7-103 to 7-108).

Interest Required on Security Deposit: Yes. (New York Consolidated General Obligation Law (GOL), Sections 7-103 to 7-108).

Separate Account required for Security Deposit: Yes. (New York Consolidated General Obligation Law (GOL), Sections 7-103 to 7-108).

Additional Security Deposit Language in Lease: None.

Exemption from Security Deposit Laws: Landlords are exempt who rent out non-regulated units in buildings with 5 or fewer units. (New York Consolidated General Obligation Law (GOL), Sections 7-103 to 7-108).

Notice Required to Change or Terminate Month-to-Month Tenancy: 1 month to terminate or change rent. (New York Consolidated Laws, Real Property Law, Section 232-a and 232-b).

Number of Days for Pay Rent or Vacate Notice: 3 days.

Rent Late Fees: No statute.

North Carolina

State Landlord-Tenant Statutes: North Carolina General Statutes, Sections 42-1 to 42-76.

State Property Laws Statutes: North Carolina General Statutes, Chapters 47B to 47F and 116A to 116B.

State Law Website: www.ncga.state.nc.us/gascripts/Statutes/StatutesTOC.pl

State Real Estate Disclosure Laws: Residential Property Disclosure Statement. (North Carolina General Statutes, Section 47E). (This form is only required for the sale of real estate).

Landlord's Entry to Real Estate: No statute.

Security Deposit Amount Limits: 1 ½ month's rent for month-to-month rental agreements. 2 month's rent if agreement is longer than 2 months. (North Carolina General Statutes, Sections 42-50 to 42-56).

Deadlines for Security Deposit Returns: 30 days. (North Carolina General Statutes, Sections 42-50 to 42-56).

Interest Required on Security Deposit: No. (North Carolina General Statutes, Sections 42-50 to 42-56).

Separate Account required for Security Deposit: Yes. (North Carolina General Statutes, Sections 42-50 to 42-56).

Additional Security Deposit Language in Lease: Yes. Must indicate in lease the name, address, and account number where the deposit funds are held.

Exemption from Security Deposit Laws: None. (North Carolina General Statutes, Sections 42-50 to 42-56).

Notice Required to Change or Terminate Month-to-Month Tenancy: 7 days to terminate or change rent. (North Carolina General Statutes, Section 42-14).

Number of Days for Pay Rent or Vacate Notice: 10 days.

Rent Late Fees: Late fee cannot exceed $15.00 or 5% of rent (whichever is greater). Landlord cannot impose this fee until rent is 5 days late. (North Carolina General Statutes, Section 42-46).

North Dakota

State Landlord-Tenant Statutes: North Dakota Century Code, Sections 47-16-01 to 47-16-41.

State Property Laws Statutes: North Dakota Century Code, Title 47.

State Law Website: www.legis.nd.gov/information/statutes/cent-code.html

State Real Estate Disclosure Laws: No statutory form.

Landlord's Entry to Real Estate: Immediate access for emergency. "Reasonable" notice required for inspection, repairs, viewing of property and entry if tenant is absent for long periods. (North Dakota Century Code, Section 47-16-07.3).

Security Deposit Amount Limits: 1 month's rent. $1,500.00 if renter has a pet. (North Dakota Century Code Section 47-16-07.1).

Deadlines for Security Deposit Returns: 30 days. (North Dakota Century Code, Section 47-16-07.1).

Interest Required on Security Deposit: Yes. (North Dakota Century Code, Section 47-16-07.1).

Separate Account required for Security Deposit: Yes. (North Dakota Century Code, Section 47-16-07.1).

Additional Security Deposit Language in Lease: None.

Exemption from Security Deposit Laws: None. (North Dakota Century Code, Section 47-16-07.1).

Notice Required to Change or Terminate Month-to-Month Tenancy: 30 days to terminate or change rent. (North Dakota Century Code, Section 47-16-15).

Number of Days for Pay Rent or Vacate Notice: 3 days.

Rent Late Fees: No statute.

Ohio

State Landlord-Tenant Statutes: Ohio Revised Code, Sections 5321.01 to 5321.19.

State Property Laws Statutes: Ohio Revised Code, Title 53.

State Law Website: onlinedocs.andersonpublishing.com/oh/lpExt.dll?f=templates&fn=titlepage.htm

State Real Estate Disclosure Laws: Residential Property Disclosure Form. (Ohio Revised Code, Section 5302.30). (This form is only required for the sale of real estate).

Landlord's Entry to Real Estate: Immediate access for emergency. 24 hour notice required for inspection, repairs, viewing of property and entry if tenant is absent for long periods. (Ohio Revised Code, Sections 5321.04(A)(8) and 5321.05(B)).

Security Deposit Amount Limits: No limit in statute. (Ohio Revised Code, Sections 5321.16).

Deadlines for Security Deposit Returns: 30 days. (Ohio Revised Code, Sections 5321.16).

Interest Required on Security Deposit: Yes. (Ohio Revised Code, Sections 5321.16).

Separate Account required for Security Deposit: No. (Ohio Revised Code, Sections 5321.16).

Additional Security Deposit Language in Lease: None.

Exemption from Security Deposit Laws: None. (Ohio Revised Code, Sections 5321.16).

Notice Required to Change or Terminate Month-to-Month Tenancy: 30 days to terminate or change rent. (Ohio Revised Code, Sections 5321.17).

Number of Days for Pay Rent or Vacate Notice: 3 days.

Rent Late Fees: No statute.

Oklahoma

State Landlord-Tenant Statutes: Oklahoma Statutes, Title 41, Sections 1-136.

State Property Laws Statutes: Oklahoma Statutes, Title 60.

State Law Website: www.oscn.net/applications/oscn/index.asp?ftdb=STOKST&level=1

State Real Estate Disclosure Laws: Residential Property Condition Disclosure Statement. (Oklahoma Statutes, Section 60-16A-831). (This form is only required for the sale of real estate).

Landlord's Entry to Real Estate: Immediate access for emergency. 1 day notice required for inspection, repairs, viewing of property. (Oklahoma Statutes, Section 41-128).

Security Deposit Amount Limits: No limit in statute. (Oklahoma Statutes, Section 41-115).

Deadlines for Security Deposit Returns: 30 days. (Oklahoma Statutes, Section 41-115).

Interest Required on Security Deposit: No. (Oklahoma Statutes, Section 41-115).

Separate Account required for Security Deposit: Yes. (Oklahoma Statutes, Section 41-115).

Additional Security Deposit Language in Lease: None.

Exemption from Security Deposit Laws: None. (Oklahoma Statutes, Section 41-115).

Notice Required to Change or Terminate Month-to-Month Tenancy: 30 days to terminate or change rent .(Oklahoma Statutes, Section 41-111).

Number of Days for Pay Rent or Vacate Notice: 5 days.

Rent Late Fees: Preset late fees are not valid. (Oklahoma Case Law).

Oregon

State Landlord-Tenant Statutes: Oregon Revised Statutes, Sections 90.100 to 90.450.

State Property Laws Statutes: Oregon Revised Statutes, Chapters 90-105.

State Law Website: landru.leg.state.or.us/ors/

State Real Estate Disclosure Laws: Seller's Property Disclosure Statement. (Oregon Revised Statutes, Section 10-105.462). (This form is only required for the sale of real estate).

Landlord's Entry to Real Estate: Immediate access for emergency. 24 hour notice required for inspection, repairs, viewing of property. (Oregon Revised Statutes, Section 90.322).

Security Deposit Amount Limits: No limit in statute. (Oregon Revised Statutes, Section 90.300).

Deadlines for Security Deposit Returns: 31 days. (Oregon Revised Statutes, Section 90.300).

Interest Required on Security Deposit: No. (Oregon Revised Statutes, Section 90.300).

Separate Account required for Security Deposit: No. (Oregon Revised Statutes, Section 90.300).

Additional Security Deposit Language in Lease: None.

Exemption from Security Deposit Laws: None. (Oregon Revised Statutes, Section 90.300).

Notice Required to Change or Terminate Month-to-Month Tenancy: 30 days to terminate or change rent. (Oregon Revised Statutes, Section 90.070).

Number of Days for Pay Rent or Vacate Notice: 10 days.

Rent Late Fees: A reasonable late fee may be charged after 5 days if specified in the lease. (Oregon Revised Statutes, Section 90.260).

Pennsylvania

State Landlord-Tenant Statutes: Pennsylvania Consolidated Statutes, Title 68, Section 250.101 to 250.510-B.

State Property Laws Statutes: Pennsylvania Consolidated Statutes, Title 68.

State Law Website: members.aol.com/StatutesPB/RecentLaws03.html

State Real Estate Disclosure Laws: Seller's Property Disclosure Statement. (Pennsylvania Consolidated Statutes, Section 68-7301). (This form is only required for the sale of real estate).

Landlord's Entry to Real Estate: No statute.

Security Deposit Amount Limits: 2 month's rent for first year, 1 month's rent for every year after. (Pennsylvania Consolidated Statutes, Sections 68-250.511a to 68-250.512).

Deadlines for Security Deposit Returns: 30 days. (Pennsylvania Consolidated Statutes, Sections 68-250.511a to 68-250.512).

Interest Required on Security Deposit: Yes. (Pennsylvania Consolidated Statutes, Sections 68-250.511a to 68-250.512).

Separate Account required for Security Deposit: Yes. (Pennsylvania Consolidated Statutes, Sections 68-250.511a to 68-250.512).

Additional Security Deposit Language in Lease: None.

Exemption from Security Deposit Laws: None. (Pennsylvania Consolidated Statutes, Sections 68-250.511a to 68-250.512).

Notice Required to Change or Terminate Month-to-Month Tenancy: No statute.

Number of Days for Pay Rent or Vacate Notice: 3 days unless a shorter time is specified in the lease.

Rent Late Fees: No statute.

Rhode Island

State Landlord-Tenant Statutes: Rhode Island General Laws, Sections 34-18-1 to 34-18-57.

State Property Laws Statutes: Rhode Island General Laws, Title 34.

State Law Website: www.rilin.state.ri.us/ Statutes/Statutes.html

State Real Estate Disclosure Laws: No statutory form. Rhode Island General Laws, Section 5-20.8-1).

Landlord's Entry to Real Estate: Immediate access for emergency. 2 days notice required for inspection, repairs, viewing of property and entry if tenant is absent for long periods. (Rhode Island General Laws Section 34-18-26).

Security Deposit Amount Limits: 1 month's rent. (Rhode Island General Laws, Section 34-18-19).

Deadlines for Security Deposit Returns: 20 days .(Rhode Island General Laws, Section 34-18-26).

Interest Required on Security Deposit: No. (Rhode Island General Laws, Section 34-18-26).

Separate Account required for Security Deposit: No .(Rhode Island General Laws, Section 34-18-26).

Additional Security Deposit Language in Lease: None.

Exemption from Security Deposit Laws: None. (Rhode Island General Laws, Section 34-18-26).

Notice Required to Change or Terminate Month-to-Month Tenancy: 30 days to terminate or change rent. (Rhode Island General Laws, Sections 34-18-16.1 and 34-18-37).

Number of Days for Pay Rent or Vacate Notice: 5 days.

Rent Late Fees: No statute.

South Carolina

State Landlord-Tenant Statutes: South Carolina Code of Laws, Sections 27-40-10 to 27-40-910.

State Property Laws Statutes: South Carolina Code of Laws, Title 27.

State Law Website: www.scstatehouse.net/code/statmast.htm

State Real Estate Disclosure Laws: Residential Property Condition Disclosure Statement. (South Carolina Code of Laws, Section 27-50-10). (This form is only required for the sale of real estate).

Landlord's Entry to Real Estate: Immediate access for emergency. 24 hour notice required for inspection, repairs, viewing of property and entry if tenant is absent for long periods. (South Carolina Code of Laws, Section 27-40-530).

Security Deposit Amount Limits: No limit in statute. (South Carolina Code of Laws, Section 27-40-410).

Deadlines for Security Deposit Returns: 30 days. (South Carolina Code of Laws, Section 27-40-410).

Interest Required on Security Deposit: No. (South Carolina Code of Laws, Section 27-40-410).

Separate Account required for Security Deposit: No .(South Carolina Code of Laws, Section 27-40-410).

Additional Security Deposit Language in Lease: None.

Exemption from Security Deposit Laws: None .(South Carolina Code of Laws, Section 27-40-410).

Notice Required to Change or Terminate Month-to-Month Tenancy: 30 days to terminate or change rent. (South Carolina Code of Laws, Section 27-40-770).

Number of Days for Pay Rent or Vacate Notice: 5 days.

Rent Late Fees: No statute.

South Dakota

State Landlord-Tenant Statutes: South Dakota Codified Laws, Sections 43-32-1 to 43-32-29.

State Property Laws Statutes: South Dakota Codified Laws, Title 43.

State Law Website: legis.state.sd.us/statutes/StatutesTitleList.aspx

State Real Estate Disclosure Laws: Seller's Property Condition Disclosure Statement. (South Dakota Codified Laws, Section 43-4-37). (This form is only required for the sale of real estate).

Landlord's Entry to Real Estate: No statute.

Security Deposit Amount Limits: 1 month's rent unless special conditions warrant more. (South Dakota Codified Laws, Sections 43-32-6.1 and 43-32-24).

Deadlines for Security Deposit Returns: 2 weeks to return entire deposit or portion with written reasons for deductions. (South Dakota Codified Laws, Sections 43-32-6.1 and 43-32-24).

Interest Required on Security Deposit: No. (South Dakota Codified Laws, Sections 43-32-6.1 and 43-32-24).

Separate Account required for Security Deposit: No. (South Dakota Codified Laws, Sections 43-32-6.1 and 43-32-24).

Additional Security Deposit Language in Lease: None.

Exemption from Security Deposit Laws: None. (South Dakota Codified Laws, Sections 43-32-6.1 and 43-32-24).

Notice Required to Change or Terminate Month-to-Month Tenancy: 1 month to terminate or change rent. Renter has 15 days to terminate after receiving landlord's modification of agreement. (South Dakota Codified Laws, Sections 43-32-13 and 43-8-8).

Number of Days for Pay Rent or Vacate Notice: 3 days.

Rent Late Fees: No statute.

Tennessee

State Landlord-Tenant Statutes: Tennessee Code, Sections 66-28-101 to 66-28-520.

State Property Laws Statutes: Tennessee Code, Title 66).

State Law Website: (select Tennessee)

State Real Estate Disclosure Laws: Residential Property Condition Disclosure. (Tennessee Code, Title 66, Chapter 5, Part 2). (This form is only required for the sale of real estate).

Landlord's Entry to Real Estate: Immediate access for emergency or abandonment. "Reasonable notice required for inspection, repairs and viewing of property. (Tennessee Code, Section 66-28-403).

Security Deposit Amount Limits: No limit in statute. (Tennessee Code, Section 66-28-301).

Deadlines for Security Deposit Returns: No deadline in statute. (Tennessee Code, Section 66-28-403).

Interest Required on Security Deposit: No. (Tennessee Code, Section 66-28-403).

Separate Account required for Security Deposit: Yes. (Tennessee Code, Section 66-28-403).

Additional Security Deposit Language in Lease: Yes. Must indicate in lease the name and address of the bank where the deposit funds will be held.

Exemption from Security Deposit Laws: None. (Tennessee Code, Section 66-28-403).

Notice Required to Change or Terminate Month-to-Month Tenancy: 30 days to terminate or change rent. (Tennessee Code, Section 66-28-512).

Number of Days for Pay Rent or Vacate Notice: 10 days.

Rent Late Fees: Landlord must wait until rent is 5 days late to impose late fee. Late fee cannot exceed 10% of the amount due. (Tennessee Code, Sections 66-28-201(d)).

Texas

State Landlord-Tenant Statutes: Texas Statutes, Property Code, Sections 91.001 - 91.006 and 92.001-92.354.

State Property Laws Statutes: Texas Statutes, Property Code.

State Law Website: www.capitol.state.tx.us/statutes/statutes.html

State Real Estate Disclosure Laws: Seller's Disclosure of Property Condition. (Texas Statutes, Property Code, Sections 5.008). (This form is only required for the sale of real estate).

Landlord's Entry to Real Estate: No statute.

Security Deposit Amount Limits: No limit in statute. (Texas Statutes, Property Code, Sections 92.101 to 92.109).

Deadlines for Security Deposit Returns: 30 days. (Texas Statutes, Property Code, Sections 92.101 to 92.109).

Interest Required on Security Deposit: No. (Texas Statutes, Property Code, Sections 92.101 to 92.109).

Separate Account required for Security Deposit: No. (Texas Statutes, Property Code, Sections 92.101 to 92.109).

Additional Security Deposit Language in Lease: None.

Exemption from Security Deposit Laws: None. Texas Statutes: (Texas Statutes, Property Code, Sections 92.101 to 92.109).

Notice Required to Change or Terminate Month-to-Month Tenancy: 1 month to terminate or change rent. (Texas Statutes, Property Code, Section 91.001).

Number of Days for Pay Rent or Vacate Notice: 3 days.

Rent Late Fees: No statute.

Utah

State Landlord-Tenant Statutes: Utah Code, Sections 57-17-1 to 57-17-5 and 57-22-1 to 57-22-6.

State Property Laws Statutes: Utah Code, Title 57.

State Law Website: www.le.state.ut.us/~code/code.htm

State Real Estate Disclosure Laws: No statutory form.

Landlord's Entry to Real Estate: Immediate access for emergency. No renter can deny access for repairs. (Utah Code, Section 57-22-5(2)(c)).

Security Deposit Amount Limits: No limit in statute. (Utah Code, Sections 57-17-1 to 57-17-5).

Deadlines for Security Deposit Returns: 30 days or 15 days after receiving tenant's forwarding address (whichever is longer). (Utah Code, Sections 57-17-1 to 57-17-5).

Interest Required on Security Deposit: No. (Utah Code, Sections 57-17-1 to 57-17-5).

Separate Account required for Security Deposit: No. (Utah Code, Sections 57-17-1 to 57-17-5).

Additional Security Deposit Language in Lease: None.

Exemption from Security Deposit Laws: None. (Utah Code, Sections 57-17-1 to 57-17-5).

Notice Required to Change or Terminate Month-to-Month Tenancy: No statute.

Number of Days for Pay Rent or Vacate Notice: 5 days.

Rent Late Fees: No statute.

Vermont

State Landlord-Tenant Statutes: Vermont Statutes, Title 9, Sections 4451 to 4468.

State Property Laws Statutes: Vermont Statutes, Title 27.

State Law Website: www.leg.state.vt.us/statutes/statutes2.htm

State Real Estate Disclosure Laws: No statutory form.

Landlord's Entry to Real Estate: Immediate access for emergency. 48 hour notice for inspection, repairs and viewing of property. (Vermont Statutes, Title 9, Section 4460).

Security Deposit Amount Limits: No limit in statute. (Vermont Statutes, Title 9, Section 4461).

Deadlines for Security Deposit Returns: 14 days. (Vermont Statutes, Title 9, Section 4461).

Interest Required on Security Deposit: No. (Vermont Statutes, Title 9, Section 4461).

Separate Account required for Security Deposit: No. (Vermont Statutes, Title 9, Section 4461).

Additional Security Deposit Language in Lease: None.

Exemption from Security Deposit Laws: None. (Vermont Statutes, Title 9, Section 4461).

Notice Required to Change or Terminate Month-to-Month Tenancy: Renter has 1 rental period to terminate or change rent. Landlord has 30 days to terminate or change rent. If there is no written agreement, the landlord has 60 days if tenant has rented for 2 years or less, 90 days if tenant has rented for more than 2 years. (Vermont Statutes, Title 9, Sections 4467 and 4456(d)).

Number of Days for Pay Rent or Vacate Notice: 14 days.

Rent Late Fees: No statute.

Virginia

State Landlord-Tenant Statutes: Code of Virginia, Sections 55-218.1 to 55-248.40.

State Property Laws Statutes: Code of Virginia, Title 55.

State Law Website: leg1.state.va.us/cgi-bin/legp504.exe?000+cod+TOC

State Real Estate Disclosure Laws: Residential Property Disclosure Statement. (Code of Virginia, Section 55-517). (This form is only required for the sale of real estate).

Landlord's Entry to Real Estate: Immediate access for emergency. 24 hours required for inspection, repairs, viewing of property and entry if tenant is absent for long periods. (Code of Virginia, Section 55-248.18).

Security Deposit Amount Limits: 2 month's rent. (Code of Virginia, Section 55-248.15: 1).

Deadlines for Security Deposit Returns: 14 days. (Code of Virginia, Section 55-248.15: 1).

Interest Required on Security Deposit: Yes. (Code of Virginia, Section 55-248.15:1).

Separate Account required for Security Deposit: No. (Code of Virginia, Section 55-248.15:1).

Additional Security Deposit Language in Lease: None.

Exemption from Security Deposit Laws: None. (Code of Virginia, Section 55-248.15: 1)..

Notice Required to Change or Terminate Month-to-Month Tenancy: 30 days to terminate or change rent. Renter must approve in writing of any change. (Code of Virginia, Sections 55-248.37 and 55-248.7).

Number of Days for Pay Rent or Vacate Notice: 5 days.

Rent Late Fees: No statute.

Washington

State Landlord-Tenant Statutes: Revised Code of Washington, Sections 59.04.010 to 59.04.900 and 59.18.010 to 59.911.

State Property Laws Statutes: Revised Code of Washington, Titles 63 and 64.

State Law Website: apps.leg.wa.gov/rcw/

State Real Estate Disclosure Laws: Seller's Residential Property Disclosures Statement. (Revised Code of Washington, Section 64.06.005). (This form is only required for the sale of real estate). Landlord's are required to provide tenants with fire and safety protection information. (Revised Code of Washington, Section 59.18.060).

Landlord's Entry to Real Estate: Immediate access for emergency. 2 days required for inspection, repairs and viewing of property. (Revised Code of Washington, Section 59.18.150).

Security Deposit Amount Limits: No limit in statutes. (Revised Code of Washington, Sections 59.18.260 to 59.18.285).

Deadlines for Security Deposit Returns: 14 days .(Revised Code of Washington, Sections 59.18.260 to 59.18.285).

Interest Required on Security Deposit: No. (Revised Code of Washington, Sections 59.18.260 to 59.18.285).

Separate Account required for Security Deposit: Yes .(Revised Code of Washington, Sections 59.18.260 to 59.18.285).

Additional Security Deposit Language in Lease: Yes. Must indicate in lease the name and address of the bank where the deposit funds will be held.

Exemption from Security Deposit Laws: None. (Revised Code of Washington, Sections 59.18.260 to 59.18.285).

Notice Required to Change or Terminate Month-to-Month Tenancy: 30 days for renter to terminate or change rent. 20 days for landlord to terminate rent and 30 days to change rent. (Revised Code of Washington, Sections 59.18.200 and 59.18.140).

Number of Days for Pay Rent or Vacate Notice: 10 days.

Rent Late Fees: No statute.

West Virginia

State Landlord-Tenant Statutes: West Virginia Code, Sections 37-6-1 to 37-6-30.

State Property Laws Statutes: West Virginia Code, Chapters 32A, 34, 35, and 36.

State Law Website: www.legis.state.wv.us/WVCODE/masterfrm3Banner.cfm

State Real Estate Disclosure Laws: No statutory form.

Landlord's Entry to Real Estate: No statute.

Security Deposit Amount Limits: No statute.

Deadlines for Security Deposit Returns: No statute.

Interest Required on Security Deposit: No statute.

Separate Account required for Security Deposit: No statute.

Additional Security Deposit Language in Lease: None.

Exemption from Security Deposit Laws: No statute.

Notice Required to Change or Terminate Month-to-Month Tenancy: 1 month to terminate or change rent. (West Virginia Code, Sections 37-6-5).

Number of Days for Pay Rent or Vacate Notice: Immediately.

Rent Late Fees: No statute.

Wisconsin

State Landlord-Tenant Statutes: Wisconsin Statutes & Annotations, Sections 704.01 to 704.45.

State Property Laws Statutes: Wisconsin Statutes & Annotations, Chapters 700-710.

State Law Website: folio.legis.state.wi.us/

State Real Estate Disclosure Laws: Real Estate Condition Report. (Wisconsin Statutes & Annotations, Section 709.01). (This form is only required for the sale of real estate).

Landlord's Entry to Real Estate: Immediate access for emergency. "Reasonable" notice required for inspection, repairs and viewing of property. (Wisconsin Statutes & Annotations, Section 704.05(2)).

Security Deposit Amount Limits: No limit in statute. (Wisconsin Administrative Code ATCP, Section 134.06).

Deadlines for Security Deposit Returns: 21 days. (Wisconsin Administrative Code ATCP, Section 134.06).

Interest Required on Security Deposit: No. (Wisconsin Administrative Code ATCP, Section 134.06).

Separate Account required for Security Deposit: No. (Wisconsin Administrative Code ATCP, Section 134.06).

Additional Security Deposit Language in Lease: None.

Exemption from Security Deposit Laws: None. (Wisconsin Administrative Code ATCP, Section 134.06).

Notice Required to Change or Terminate Month-to-Month Tenancy: 28 days to terminate or change rent. (Wisconsin Statutes & Annotations, Sections 704.19).

Number of Days for Pay Rent or Vacate Notice: 14 days if rent is late for 2nd time within 1 year under a year-to-year lease. 30 days to terminate a lease for unpaid rent if lease is for over 1 year.

Rent Late Fees: No statute.

Wyoming

State Landlord-Tenant Statutes: Wyoming Statutes, Sections 1-21-1201 to 1-21-1211 and 34-2-128 to 34-2-129.

State Property Laws Statutes: Wyoming Statutes, Title 34.

State Law Website: legisweb.state.wy.us/statutes/statutes.htm

State Real Estate Disclosure Laws: No statutory form.

Landlord's Entry to Real Estate: No statute.

Security Deposit Amount Limits: No limit in statute. (Wyoming Statutes, Sections 1-21-1207 to 1-21-1208).

Deadlines for Security Deposit Returns: 30 days or 15 days after receiving renter's forwarding address (whichever is later). 60 days if there are deductions for damages .(Wyoming Statutes, Sections 1-21-1207 to 1-21-1208).

Interest Required on Security Deposit: No. (Wyoming Statutes, Sections 1-21-1207 to 1-21-1208).

Separate Account required for Security Deposit: No. (Wyoming Statutes, Sections 1-21-1207 to 1-21-1208).

Additional Security Deposit Language in Lease: None.

Exemption from Security Deposit Laws: None. (Wyoming Statutes, Sections 1-21-1207 to 1-21-1208).

Notice Required to Change or Terminate Month-to-Month Tenancy: No statute.

Number of Days for Pay Rent or Vacate Notice: 3 days.

Rent Late Fees: No statute.

Index

★ Nova Publishing Company ★
Small Business and Consumer Legal Books and Software

Law Made Simple Series

Estate Planning Simplified
ISBN 1-892949-10-5	Book w/Forms-on-CD	$34.95

Living Trusts Simplified
ISBN 0-935755-53-5	Book only	$22.95
ISBN 0-935755-51-9	Book w/Forms-on-CD	$28.95

Living Wills Simplified
ISBN 0-935755-52-7	Book only	$22.95
ISBN 0-935755-50-0	Book w/Forms-on-CD	$28.95

Personal Legal Forms Simplified (3rd Edition)
ISBN 0-935755-97-7	Book w/Forms-on-CD	$28.95

Small Business Made Simple Series

Corporation: Small Business Start-up Kit (2nd Edition)
ISBN 1-892949-06-7	Book w/Forms-on-CD	$29.95

Limited Liability Company: Small Business Start-up Kit (3rd Edition)
ISBN 978-1-892949-37-0	Book w/Forms-on-CD	$29.95

Partnership: Small Business Start-up Kit (2nd Edition)
ISBN 1-892949-07-5	Book w/Forms-on-CD	$29.95

Real Estate Forms Simplified
ISBN 1-892949-09-1	Book w/Forms-on-CD	$29.95

S-Corporation: Small Business Start-up Kit (2nd Edition)
ISBN 1-892949-05-9	Book w/Forms-on-CD	$29.95

Small Business Accounting Simplified (4th Edition)
ISBN 1-892949-17-2	Book only	$24.95

Small Business Bookkeeping Systems Simplified
ISBN 0-935755-74-8	Book only	$14.95

Small Business Legal Forms Simplified (4th Edition)
ISBN 0-935755-98-5	Book w/Forms-on-CD	$29.95

Small Business Payroll Systems Simplified
ISBN 0-935755-55-1	Book only	$14.95

Sole Proprietorship: Small Business Start-up Kit (2nd Edition)
ISBN 1-892949-08-3	Book w/Forms-on-CD	$29.95

Legal Self-Help Series

Divorce Yourself: The National No-Fault Divorce Kit (6th Edition)
ISBN 1-892949-11-3	Book only	$29.95
ISBN 1-892949-12-1	Book w/Forms-on-CD	$39.95
ISBN 1-892949-13-X	Forms-on-CD only	$12.95

Incorporate Now!: The National Corporation Kit (4th Edition)
ISBN 1-892949-00-8	Book w/Forms-on-CD	$29.95

Prepare Your Own Will: The National Will Kit (6th Edition)
ISBN 1-892949-14-8	Book only	$19.95
ISBN 1-892949-15-6	Book w/Forms-on-CD	$29.95

National Legal Kits

Simplified Divorce Kit (2nd Edition)
ISBN 1-892949-20-2	Book only	$19.95

Simplified Family Legal Forms Kit
ISBN 1-892949-18-0	Book only	$18.95

Simplified Living Will Kit
ISBN 1-892949-22-9	Book only	$15.95

Simplified Will Kit (3rd Edition)
ISBN 978-1-892949-38-7	Kit w/Forms-on-CD	$19.95

Simplified S-Corporation Kit
ISBN 1-892949-31-8	Kit w/Forms-on-CD	$19.95

Simplified Limited Limited Liability Kit
ISBN 1-892949-32-6	Kit w/Forms-on-CD	$19.95

Simplified Incorporation Kit
ISBN 978-1-892949-33-2	Kit w/Forms-on-CD	$19.95

☆ Ordering Information ☆

Distributed by:
National Book Network
4501 Forbes Blvd. Suite 200
Lanham MD 20706

Shipping: $4.50 for first & $.75 for each additional
Phone orders with Visa/MC: (800) 462-6420
Fax orders with Visa/MC: (800) 338-4550
Internet: www.novapublishing.com
Free shipping on all internet orders